That They May All Be One

That They May All Be One

*Celebrating the World Communion
of Reformed Churches*

Essays in Honor of Clifton Kirkpatrick

Edited by
NEAL D. PRESA

WESTMINSTER
JOHN KNOX PRESS
LOUISVILLE • KENTUCKY

First edition
Published by Westminster John Knox Press
Louisville, Kentucky

10 11 12 13 14 15 16 17 18 19—10 9 8 7 6 5 4 3 2 1

Except as otherwise noted, Scripture quotations are from the New Revised Standard Version of the Bible, copyright © 1989 by the Division of Christian Education of the National Council of the Churches of Christ in the U.S.A., and used by permission. Versions briefly cited: NKJV, New King James Version; TNIV, Today's New International Version.

"Covenant for Life in Creation" from the report Covenanting to Live Faithfully in the Midst of Empire, The United Church of Canada, General Council 2009. Reprinted with permission.

"A Common Word between Us and You" is edited and reprinted with permission of the editor of *The Presbyterian Outlook.*

Book design by Sharon Adams
Cover design by Night & Day Design

Library of Congress Cataloging-in-Publication Data

That they may all be one : celebrating the world communion of reformed churches : essays in honor of Clifton Kirkpatrick / Neal D. Presa, editor.
　　p. cm.
　ISBN 978-0-664-23572-7 (alk. paper)
　1. Interdenominational cooperation.　2. Missions—Interdenominational cooperation.
3. Christianity and justice.　I. Presa, Neal D.　II. Kirkpatrick, Clifton, 1945–
　BV625.T44 2010
　266'.42—dc22

2010003666

PRINTED IN THE UNITED STATES OF AMERICA

⊗ The paper used in this publication meets the minimum requirements
of the American National Standard for Information Sciences—Permanence
of Paper for Printed Library Materials, ANSI Z39.48-1992.

Westminster John Knox Press advocates the responsible use of our natural resources. The text paper of this book is made from 30% postconsumer waste.

Dedicated to
Clifton Kirkpatrick,
ecumenist, servant leader, mentor, colleague, friend

For his years of extraordinary and outstanding leadership
in the ecumenical movement,
the World Council of Churches,
President of the World Alliance of Reformed Churches,
the National Council of Churches of Christ (U.S.A.),
Stated Clerk Emeritus and Global Missions Director of
the Presbyterian Church (U.S.A.)

Contents

PART 4. FOR SUCH A TIME AS THIS:
NEW DIRECTIONS IN ECUMENISM AND MISSION

About the Contributors

Scott Anderson, executive director, Wisconsin Council of Churches

His Holiness Aram I, Catholicos of the See of Cilicia of the Armenian Apostolic Church (Antelias, Lebanon); past moderator, Central Committee, World Council of Churches

Omega Bula, executive minister, Justice, Global and Ecumenical Relations Unit, United Church of Canada

Cynthia M. Campbell, president and Cyrus McCormick Professor of Church and Ministry, McCormick Theological Seminary (Chicago); former chair, Presbyterian Church General Assembly Committee on the Consultation on Church Union

Anna Case-Winters, Professor of Theology, McCormick Theological Seminary; cochair, International Commission for Lutheran-Reformed Relations; former moderator of the Theology Committee, Caribbean and North American Area Council, World Alliance of Reformed Churches

Edward Chan, past chair of the General Assembly Committee on Ecumenical Relations, Presbyterian Church (U.S.A.)

Jane Dempsey Douglass, Hazel Thompson McCord Professor of Historical Theology Emerita, Princeton Theological Seminary; former vice president and president, World Alliance of Reformed Churches

Hunter Farrell, Director of World Mission, Presbyterian Church (U.S.A.)

Wesley Granberg-Michaelson, general secretary, Reformed Church in America; a President of Christian Churches Together (CCT-USA); Steering Committee, Global Christian Forum

Bernice Powell Jackson, president (North America area), World Council of Churches

Roberto Jordan, minister member, Reformed Churches in Argentina; member, Executive Committee, World Alliance of Reformed Churches

Michael Kinnamon, general secretary, National Council of Churches of Christ (U.S.A.); former Allen and Dottie Miller Professor of Mission and Peace, Eden Theological Seminary (St. Louis); former general secretary, Consultation on Church Union; former executive secretary, Faith and Order Commission, World Council of Churches

Clifton Kirkpatrick, president, World Alliance of Reformed Churches; stated clerk emeritus, Presbyterian Church (U.S.A.)

Samuel Kobia, general secretary, World Council of Churches (2004–2009)

Lew Lancaster, former ecumenical officer of the Presbyterian Church (U.S.A.) and former acting general secretary, Consultation on Church Union

Aimee Moiso, Campus Ministry Director for Ecumenical and Interfaith Ministries, Santa Clara University; Presbyterian Church (U.S.A.) delegate to General Assembly of the National Council of Churches of Christ (U.S.A.), and vice-chair of Faith and Order Commission of the NCCC-USA

Setri Nyomi, general secretary, World Alliance of Reformed Churches

Ofelia Ortega, former principal, Evangelical Theological Seminary, Matanzas, Cuba; President (Latin America area), World Council of Churches; vice president/moderator for Theology, Ecumenical Engagement and Communion, World Alliance of Reformed Churches

Kathleen Cook Owens, chair, Consultation on the Ecumenical Stance of the Presbyterian Church (U.S.A.), and member, General Assembly Committee on Ecumenical Relations, Presbyterian Church (U.S.A.)

Gradye Parsons, stated clerk of the Presbyterian Church (U.S.A.)

Rebecca Todd Peters, associate professor and chair of Department of Religious Studies, Elon University (Elon, N.C.); member, Faith and Order Standing and Plenary Commission, World Council of Churches; Presbyterian Church (U.S.A.) delegate to General Assembly of the National Council of Churches of Christ (U.S.A.)

Neal D. Presa, convenor/chair, Caribbean and North American Area Council and corresponding member, Executive Committee, World Alliance of Reformed Churches; Presbyterian Church (U.S.A.) delegate to Uniting General Council of the World Communion of Reformed Churches

Joseph D. Small, director, Theology Worship and Education, General Assembly Mission Council, Presbyterian Church (U.S.A.); cochair, Reformed-Pentecostal bilateral dialogues

Iain Torrance, president and Professor of Patristics, Princeton Theological Seminary, a former moderator of the Church of Scotland and a Chaplain-in-Ordinary to HM Queen Elizabeth II; cochair, Reformed-Eastern Orthodox bilateral dialogues

Eugene Turner, former associate stated clerk for Ecumenical and Agency Relations, Presbyterian Church (U.S.A.)

Richard van Houten, general secretary of the Reformed Ecumenical Council

Douwe Visser, executive secretary for Theology and Ecumenical Engagement, World Alliance of Reformed Churches; former president of the Reformed Ecumenical Council

Philip Wickeri, Flora Lamson Hewlett Professor of Evangelism and Mission, San Francisco Theological Seminary; dean, Global Theological Institute, 24th General Council, World Alliance of Reformed Churches (Accra, Ghana); former chair, General Assembly Committee on Ecumenical Relations of the Presbyterian Church (U.S.A.)

Greetings from World Church Leaders

On many occasions in the past, we had the opportunity to meet Dr. Kirkpatrick in the framework of various interchurch gatherings and to appreciate the gentle, but competent and efficacious way in which he dealt with major and delicate issues affecting the ecumenical movement today. We are particularly grateful to him for the attention and respect he has always manifested to his Orthodox interlocutors, as well as for his support to the ongoing theological dialogue between World Alliance of Reformed Churches (WARC) and the entire Orthodox Church.

May our Lord Jesus Christ grant him health, strength, and long life, in order to continue his ministry, with the same dedication and the same fervor, for the glory of God and the advance of the common effort for Christian Unity.

Wishing you all good things, we bestow upon you and your colleagues in WARC our Patriarchal blessings.

> At the Patriarchate, 24th of June 2009
> Your fervent supplicant before God,
> Bartholomew
> Archbishop of Constantinople,
> New Rome and Ecumenical Patriarch

For many years Rev. Dr. Kirkpatrick has been a wise and conscientious partner in ecumenical relations. He has always kept at the forefront of his ministry his faith in Jesus Christ and a commitment to Christian unity, so "that they may all be one, . . . that the world may believe" (John 17:21). As he completes his term as president of WARC, we at the Pontifical Council for Promoting Christian Unity are deeply grateful for his friendship and the many occasions we have had to work together. May the Lord continue to bless his ministry and his life.

Cardinal Walter Kasper
President
Pontifical Council for Promoting Christian Unity

Visionary leadership is what drives the ecumenical movement, leadership rooted in Jesus' prayer in St. John's Gospel, and a passion to further God's mission in the world. Such a figure is Rev. Dr. Clifton Kirkpatrick. Strongly rooted in his own Reformed tradition, he has engaged that tradition in the common striving for the visible expression of our oneness in Christ, and through his leadership much progress has been made. We thank God for him, for his ministry, his witness, and his service, and wish him God's blessing in retirement.

The Reverend Canon Kenneth Kearon
Secretary General of the Anglican Communion
(on behalf of The Archbishop of Canterbury)

I cherish the fond memory of your gesture of ecumenical friendship when I was leaving my mandate of General Secretary of the World Council of Churches (WCC). Therefore I want to seize the opportunity of expressing to you my deep appreciation for your long and dedicated service to the ecumenical movement, both at home and on the worldwide level. During the period of your presidency of the WARC, you guided the Alliance through at least two very significant processes, the Accra meeting of the General Council, with its prophetic statement on globalization; and the bringing together of the Alliance and the Reformed Ecumenical Council. We all have received significant inspiration from you, and I will always be grateful for the personal support and encouragement that you have given to me.

May God continue to bless you as you prepare for a new period of life in which you are liberated from institutional responsibilities and constraints.

In friendship yours
Konrad Raiser
Former WCC General Secretary
(1993–2003)

I send greetings to Dr. Kirkpatrick as he comes to the end of his term as WARC president. Dr Kirkpatrick has given impressive leadership both within his own church and also within the wider ecumenical movement, in the United States and on the world stage. His contribution to the work of the World Council of Churches and in particular his contribution to the Central Committee has been important and an inspiration to many. May his vision and commitment to the visible unity of the church be passed on to those in the Reformed tradition and to others in the ecumenical movement.

> Dame Mary Tanner
> WCC President for Europe

It was my good fortune to work with you in WCC committees between 1998 and 2006, where your knowledge, experience, and commitment to ecumenism along with your innate wisdom were invaluable. In the midst of often difficult discussions, you spoke to the point with contributions that brought new perspectives to the situation. Your friendly, good-natured approach made you a delight to be with. Blessings in your retirement.

> Marion Best
> Vice Moderator of WCC Central Committee
> (1998–2006)

I have come to know Clifton Kirkpatrick as a person who is deeply committed to the Lord we serve, to the Reformed heritage we share, and to the gift of unity the global church has received. Clifton's efforts of many years to encourage a greater expression of that unity among all of God's people is both an inspiration and model for all who have walked that journey with him. There is no greater honor we can bestow on this servant of God than to affirm his significant contribution to the advancement of the name of Jesus Christ as the head of the church. The formation of the World Communion of Reformed Churches is a marvelous testimony to Clifton's efforts on behalf of us all.

> The Rev. Dr. Peter Borgdorff
> President of the Reformed Ecumenical Council
> and Executive Director-Emeritus of the
> Christian Reformed Church of North America

I met Clifton Kirkpatrick in Geneva about the Calvin Jubilee in 2007. His stature and his title were impressive! Warm and direct personality, he was the bridge between the old Reformed churches in Europe and the Presbyterian churches of America and the unifier of the Reformed churches around the world. Thanks, dear Clifton, for what you did for the Jubilee. I rejoice to exchange with you about this wonderful project.

> Charlotte Kuffer
> President, Protestant Church of Geneva

The ecumenical movement at all levels, in all times and places could count on Cliff Kirkpatrick. Dr. Kirkpatrick not only believed in the unity of the church and the renewal of our human community. He also lived it. I have known Cliff for nearly thirty years. His steady, visionary leadership piloted the ecumenical ship over treacherous waters. Those of us in leadership remain eternally grateful for his courage and commitment.

> Rev. Dr. Joan Brown Campbell
> Former General Secretary
> National Council of Churches of Christ, USA
> (1991–99)

Dear Cliff,

What a joy it is to join so many others in honoring [Cliff's] singular commitment to the unity of the body of Christ, expressed through your decades of service to the Presbyterian Church, the World Alliance of Reformed Churches, and the World Council of Churches. True to the gospel of Christ, to the Reformed Tradition, and to the ecumenical movement, you have lived and served the one God, who created all the earth and this wonderfully diverse humanity that is the human family. From our work together within the Presbyterian and Reformed family and in the ecumenical life of the NCC, I have been honored to know you and to call you friend, brother, and colleague. Thank you for your generous spirit, your personal support and friendship, your ecumenical heart, and your steadfast endurance along our arduous journey into the unity already given us in the very fabric of creation. Grace and peace, now and always.

> Rev. Michael E. Livingston
> Immediate Past President
> National Council of Churches of Christ, USA
> (2006–7)

Editor's Preface

*I*n his commentaries on Jesus' priestly prayer for unity in John 17:21 ("that they may all be one"), John Calvin observed:

> He again lays down the end of our happiness as consisting in unity, and justly; for the ruin of the human race is, that, having been alienated from God, it is also broken and scattered in itself. The restoration of it, therefore, on the contrary, consists in its being properly united in one body, as Paul declares the perfection of the Church to consist in believers being joined together in one spirit and says that apostles, prophets, evangelists, and pastors were given, that they might edify and restore the body of Christ, till it came to the unity of faith.[1]

He goes on to say:

> Wherefore, whenever Christ speaks about unity, let us remember how basely and shockingly, when separated from him, the world is scattered; and, next, let us learn that the commencement of a blessed life is, that we be all governed, and that we all live, by the Spirit of Christ alone.

When we speak of a blessed and happy life, if we heed the comments of the Genevan Reformer, we are to be restless and all the while uncomfortable so long as there is this scattering and disunity in the human family, most especially the brokenness and fragmentation that plagues the body of Christ, a division that the Reformed tradition is far too familiar with over the last five hundred years.

The inauguration of the World Communion of Reformed Churches in Grand Rapids, Michigan, in June 2010, with the union of the World Alliance of Reformed Churches and the Reformed Ecumenical Council, marks an important milestone in the modern ecumenical movement for visible unity in the body of Christ, expressing our common faith as people of God and a joint commitment to work for justice in the world.

What is being celebrated and inaugurated is a communion of churches. While discussions continue around what is meant by such a designation, what remains clear from our Lord's prayer in John's Gospel, as well as Calvin's comments on it, is this notion that the Trinitarian oneness of the Father, the Son, and the Holy Spirit—in essence, in work, in function, in goal (or to put it more colloquially, oneness in heart, mind, and spirit)—is being prayed for by our Lord upon all of God's people so that this oneness of heart, mind, and spirit will govern our thoughts, actions, and words with one another and in the world.

The church is not the Trinity, and so therefore we will never be uniform in our beliefs and actions. But Jesus' priestly prayer, far from calling for the total uniformity and unity that belongs solely to the Godhead, seeks a common witness whereby the gathering of God's people will be such that, when the world sees us, it will observe a people passionate about feeding the poor, freeing the oppressed, caring for the widows and orphans, speaking truth to powers and principalities, teaching and modeling Christ's kingdom ethics to the next generation.

This volume seeks to advance the conversation of what it means to live into communion for the sake of justice in the world, working for the visible unity of the people of God, and giving the common expression of faith that has already been gifted to us by the triune God. The challenge before the World Communion of Reformed Churches is also a grand opportunity for our collective reflection and action: how do we genuinely live out the call to be a communion of churches for the sake of justice in the world today? We will gather in Grand Rapids under the theme "Unity of the Spirit in the Bond of Peace." Only by and through God's Spirit will the communion that we pray for and work toward be realized. May it be so!

To begin that conversation, the twenty-seven contributors in this book approach that question from the angles of mission, justice, and ecumenism. I am grateful to all of them for their thoughtful pieces, for giving careful attention to the subject, for their participation in this project, and for the servant leadership they each and all lend in their diverse ministry contexts for the visible unity of the body of Christ.

A project such as this takes a communion of friends to refine, implement, and see it through. Four of us, Setri Nyomi, Gradye Parsons, Robina Winbush, and I managed and coedited this project in gratitude to God for the gifts Clifton Kirkpatrick has offered the ecumenical family through his leadership of the Presbyterian Church (U.S.A.) and the World Alliance of Reformed

Churches. We do so on behalf of the WARC, CANAAC, and the PC(USA). Thanks are due to Penny Blachut for providing administrative assistance; to the WARC Secretariat for providing funding; to Geneva Press and its executive director and my friend, David Maxwell, for shepherding it through the approval, editing, and publishing process. On a personal note, I thank my wife, Grace, and sons, Daniel and Andrew, for letting me take on this project in the midst of everything else on our plate.

It is very fitting that as we speak of communion and justice, a worldwide community of friends, co-laborers, and colleagues join us in dedicating this volume to Clifton Kirkpatrick, stated clerk emeritus of the Presbyterian Church (U.S.A.) and president of the World Alliance of Reformed Churches, who has been a tireless leader and advocate for the unity of God's people. May God richly bless you, Cliff, and the World Communion of Reformed Churches.

Neal D. Presa, Editor
Middlesex, New Jersey
July 20, 2009
Soli Deo gloria

Abbreviations

AGAPE	Alternative Globalization Addressing Peoples and Earth
COCU	Consultation on Church Union
CofE	Church of England
CUIC	Churches Uniting in Christ
IMF	International Monetary Fund
KJV	King James Version
NAE	National Association of Evangelicals
NCC	National Council of Churches
NCCC-USA	National Council of the Churches of Christ, USA
NGO	nongovernmental organization
NKJV	New King James Version
PC(USA)	Presbyterian Church (U.S.A.)
REC	Reformed Ecumenical Council
STM	short-term mission
TNIV	Today's New International Version
UN	United Nations
WARC	World Alliance of Reformed Churches
WCC	World Council of Churches
WCRC	World Communion of Reformed Churches
WTO	World Trade Organization

PART 1   *Missio Dei*
and *Missa Ecclesiae*

On Mission

Chapter 1

Koinōnia and Mission

RICHARD L. VAN HOUTEN

And we evangelicals always start with *martyria* at the heart of mission."
These words were dropped almost casually by Dr. Thomas Schirrmacher at a
meeting on Christian-Muslim dialogue in October 2008. Schirrmacher, who
represented the World Evangelical Alliance, evoked not only the original
meaning of *martyria*, "witness," but also signaled the sense of *martyr*, its
English derivative. Indeed, in recent decades the World Evangelical Alliance
has raised its profile of advocacy and defense of Christians who endure persecution for the sake of the gospel. Coming from a tradition in which mission
has been mostly proclamation of the gospel, these words are a sign of major
shifts taking place in the evangelical community.

Classically, *martyria* has been the central theme of mission in church
history. Such witness was expressed in proclamation (*kerygma*), service
(*diakonia*), and fellowship (*koinōnia*). It is no secret that the modern mission enterprise, begun in the late eighteenth century, focused first with proclamation. Not long into that enterprise, there were also people for whom
service was the primary vehicle of witness. Perhaps frustrated by the lack
of response or even opposition to proclamation, they turned to a witness by
service. Doctors and teachers were frequently on the vanguard of Western
missions, with service as their vehicle of witness. Few in the beginning,
however, saw *koinōnia* as a major expression of witness. A little further
in mission history, there were some who argued for a witness of presence.
"Let them see how we live, and they will believe." However, this was often
an example of *koinōnia* among the missionaries, not in the whole Christian
community. The agents of mission surely experienced profound fellowship with those among whom they worked. Still, it was mainly a movement
from "us" to "them," and when, by God's grace, "they" became "us," we in

3

"sending" churches moved our relationship down and went in search of a new "them" to evangelize.

In a sense, much of church history in the twentieth century was a gradual shift of that pattern, beginning with the formation of the International Missionary Council in 1921. Through this and other ecumenical efforts, the church clearly identified itself as a mission body and began the journey to recognize the worldwide nature of the church.

It has been mainly through the ecumenical movement, in all its varied dimensions and vehicles, that the church has explored what *koinōnia* means for mission. This exploration has gone through various phases, such as the debate about having a moratorium on sending missionaries. Churches also discussed the sharing of responsibility to conduct mission activities, through roundtable decision making by equal partners in organizations such as the Council for World Mission. When the International Missionary Council joined the World Council of Churches in 1961, its action recognized the engagement of the churches in mission through its ecumenical efforts.

Ecumenical bodies by their nature are focused on the unity of the church. Most have the promotion of unity as their primary aim. The mission movement had no small role in bringing this motive to the agenda of the churches. Many in the mission movement found the fragmentation of the church, particularly the Protestant wing, scandalous. Fragmentation and division compromised witness. While missionaries occasionally found tools for promoting unity in the areas of proclamation and service, it was the area of fellowship that received the most attention.

Communion is another translation for *koinōnia*, one that has surfaced at several points in the ecumenical world. In the 1980s, groups of churches organized around common traditions changed their self-description from world confessional families to Christian world communions. Several of these bodies now label themselves communions. The Anglicans call themselves a communion, and the Lutheran World Federation has declared that it forms a communion. Likewise, in the union of the World Alliance of Reformed Churches and the Reformed Ecumenical Council scheduled for 2010, the new body will be named the World Communion of Reformed Churches. It is appropriate to record, in this book dedicated to Clifton Kirkpatrick, that in the small committee that first proposed the union, he was the one who first suggested that it be called a "communion." That suggestion received rapid acceptance in the small group, but the word's definition and impact are still being explored as the two groups move toward union.

A new community for those who believe is one of the great promises of the gospel. In Christ, we would no longer be Jew or Gentile, male or female, slave or free. The barrier wall in the temple that kept even the God-fearers (converted Gentiles) from the courts where Jews could enter was now broken. Then, seeing how the new group lived was a powerful witness to the rest of the community. And a great deal of the New Testament teaching was about how to be a new community.

In traditional mission, however, community did not take its rightful place. In my own mission orientation in 1982, I remember asking about dealing with the disparity of being a North American in a country of the global South. How could we deal with the comparative difference in our wealth—which was small by North American standards, but large almost everywhere else—and those of our colleagues with whom we worked? One of the answers I received was to provide hospitality. Live relatively simply (even if that was sumptuous by local standards), but share what you have. In the end, that simple answer addressed only personal ethics, without dealing with the differences we have. I found a moment of truth in that answer. I wonder whether I would have survived in Hong Kong without a large apartment to return to and the money to buy food that was familiar enough. In the stress of living, having a place to relax was important. I justified my status by saying that I was more productive in my work because I had the tools to live and survive. At the same time, I asked myself if I was truly committed to building community. If I was, would I not have made the sacrifices to live as one of my colleagues? I was productive, but was I a good witness, a good martyr?

This is a well-known missionary issue. Some have advocated immersion strategies. Go to a new place, live with a local person, eat only the local food, and hear only the local language. I heard of some who tried this in Hong Kong, but their partners in Hong Kong were so concerned about them that they put them up with a wealthy Hong Kong family. The newly arrived missionary lived in greater luxury than any of the rest of the missionary community there. Moreover, the elite Hong Kong family spoke as much English as they did Cantonese.

Global disparities in wealth are indeed one of the great obstacles to community. We could all live with some differences, as long as the poorest among us still had a place to live, clothes to wear, and food to eat. But the vast differences between the poor and the rich in this world are a scandal to the Christian claim to form a new community.

The church, often through ecumenical organizations, has addressed this problem from several angles. We have had debates about sharing. We wanted the sharing to be mutual in some way, but we had trouble identifying how it could be mutual when one side seemed to possess all the riches. In mutual sharing, each side had to bring something to the table. Some from the global South suggested they could bring spirituality because they had made innovations in worship. However, pious Christians from the global North felt insulted that their spirituality was being called into question. We have become more innovative in this ongoing discussion. Among other ideas, we have begun naming the experience of suffering as something the global South brings to the North.[1]

Another approach has been to address the difference as a structural economic issue. Ecumenical bodies have made many calls about injustices in various aspects of the economic system. They have pointed to the havoc wreaked by international currency exchanges and have campaigned against unjust debt and trade agreements, just to name a few. The World Evangelical Alliance has launched a campaign, the Micah Challenge, to mobilize different Christian groups in support of the United Nations Millennium Development Goals. The World Alliance of Reformed Churches worked for a decade to develop the Accra Confession, which declared such international economic injustice an affront to the Christian faith. The WARC seeks to make this confession a matter of such deep justice that it calls for confession of wrong. Each of these initiatives has been warmly received by some Christians in the global South as well as the North, but nothing has won wide acceptance yet.

Yet another approach toward exploring communion has come through the ideas of partnership. Clearly, partnership is part of communion. It is relationship building, and the word "partner" suggests that there is a sharing, and in some way, an equal sharing in the common ministry. In the Reformed Ecumenical Council, this is one area we have explored as we tried to deal with sharing within our communion.[2] Partnering has lately become a thin idea. One definition we could suggest is the accomplishment of a goal by two or more parties that none of them could accomplish on their own. This has a strong contractual sense, where we name a specific goal and name what each partner will bring to the table to achieve that goal. Good partnerships have measureable goals and a clear time frame, as would a contract. There may be a good working relationship, and an effective outcome, but where is the communion? Where is the recognition of one another as brothers and sisters?

Though partnership has need for some clear understandings, and these take on the contractual elements of documents such as a memorandum of understanding, partnership has a more profound and durable essence. A few years ago, when I started a survey of all the mission partnerships within the REC family, we listed possible ways of partnership, such as block grants, specific projects, long-term and short-term resident missionary presence. We added to that list ecclesiastical recognition. In ecumenical work, we often see ecclesiastical recognition as a kind of flowering or completion of a mission enterprise. Many of our members are churches that were founded through a mission work of one of our other members. Gaining membership in the REC for the new church was one of the ways the mission-sending church led it into a fuller church life. Once the mission-receiving church established a full synod or general assembly, they also received mutual ecclesiastical recognition, which usually was formalized as pulpit and table fellowship.

These latter kinds of partnerships differ from the earlier relations in that they were not time bound. Membership in an ecumenical body is not for a specific time period; it stretches indefinitely into the future. The same is true of ecclesiastical fellowship. Block grants, projects, and missionary presence are typically time limited, however. In fact, most mission-sending churches mark their success by phasing out their mission work. In his study,[3] Roland Hoksbergen pointed out that the partner churches from the global South do not understand this attitude. Hoksbergen advised the churches of the North to "phase out, phase out." In other words, stop thinking about partnerships as term projects.

Certainly the terms and activities within a partnership will vary over time. A partnership without end has to guard against the pitfall of dependency, but if partnership is really a dimension of *koinōnia*, of fellowship, we must begin to think of it as stretching toward eternity. We may worry about dependency, but perhaps a greater sin is independency. We are a community. We are a family, all brothers and sisters in Christ. We want to see each other strong, healthy, and mutually caring. We will not get there by increasing our isolation, but we will meet our responsibilities to each other more fully through deep partnerships with one another.

As each brings gifts and resources to the partners' table, we may have an avenue to address the injustices, the economic disparities, and the varying maturity in Christ's body. God promises that he has given great gifts to his people, gifts so that all may work together in the unity of the faith.

> The gifts he gave were that some would be apostles, some prophets, some evangelists, some pastors and teachers, [12]to equip the saints for the work of ministry, for building up the body of Christ, [13]until all of us come to the unity of the faith and of the knowledge of the Son of God, to maturity, to the measure of the full stature of Christ. [14]We must no longer be children, tossed to and fro and blown about by every wind of doctrine, by people's trickery, by their craftiness in deceitful scheming. [15]But speaking the truth in love, we must grow up in every way into him who is the head, into Christ, [16]from whom the whole body, joined and knitted together by every ligament with which it is equipped, as each part is working properly, promotes the body's growth in building itself up in love. (*Eph. 4:11–16*)

Chapter 2

Never Let a Crisis Go to Waste

SCOTT D. ANDERSON

*R*ahm Emanuel, President Barack Obama's chief of staff, coined the phrase when he served in Congress: "Never let a crisis go to waste." However dire the situation, there are always opportunities to seize.

The same is true for U.S. mainline Protestant Churches as they face their most dire situation in over a century. Faced with staggering membership losses, the demise of national church structures, and marginalization in the wider culture, the Holy Spirit is still actively at work in our midst. We cannot let this crisis go to waste!

An Opportunity to Revisit Our Ecclesiology

For much of the last three hundred years, Western mission was largely a European-church-centered enterprise. The gospel to which we testified around the world had been passed along in the cultural shape of the Western church. This church was the result of centuries of the Western cultural tradition that we now define as "Christendom."

A paradigm shift has occurred in the last sixty years. The new missiological consensus, articulated most persuasively by Bishop Lesslie Newbigin, is summarized by the term, *missio Dei*, "mission of God." The former ecclesiocentric understanding of mission has been replaced in the last six decades by a profoundly theocentric reconceptualization of Christian mission. We have come to see that mission is not merely an activity of the church. Rather, mission is the result of God's initiative, rooted in God's purposes to restore and heal creation. We have learned to speak of God as the missionary God. And thus we have learned to understand the church as a "sent people."

Bishop Newbigin and other ecumenical missiologists have helped us see that God's mission is calling and sending the church of Jesus Christ to be a missionary church in our own societies, in the cultures and subcultures in which we find ourselves. In 1986, Newbigin posed the question "Can the West be converted?" He understood that Western nations, formerly and commonly considered to be Christian, no longer were so. Now their character as mission fields has become obvious.

Thus the opportunity before the churches in the United States is their faithful response to this challenge of moving from an ecclesiocentric missiology toward a missional ecclesiology, or in simpler terms, from "church with mission" to "missional church."

An Opportunity for Death and Resurrection

The recent experience of the stodgy, ossified Church of England (CofE) points to the possibilities of new life in the midst of denominational death. The Church of England, which is now missing two generations of churchgoers, actually has identified an official date for its denominational funeral service: 2033.

The CofE's sense of desperation about its own survival is motivating it to think completely outside the box and giving it permission to develop a culture of experimentation to engage its twenty-first-century mission field. Finding that its traditional church-planting methodology was a dismal failure, the CofE has borrowed insights from the global church and the emergent church movement in the United States to develop eleven models of church planting and revitalization. In its theological framework and among its key leadership, it has fully embraced contextualization—not presupposing what "church" is going to look like in any particular context—and is on the way to meeting its denominational goal of initiating ten thousand "fresh expressions" of church by 2014.

The comparatively stronger churched culture of the United States leaves the mainline American churches acting as if business-oriented attractional strategies of church growth will save us. If current patterns of decline continue, the U.S. churches are probably ten to fifteen years behind the Church of England. The opportunity for American church leaders is to be proactive and intentional about our missional future while there is still some semblance of institutional capacity. Otherwise, we will wait for desperation to be the motivating factor for change.

An Opportunity to Move from "Top Down" to "Bottom Up"

The midlevel judicatory is rapidly becoming the new denomination, taking on responsibilities and developing systems that used to be the purview of national church structures. Judicatories that are at the forefront of reclaiming a missional ecclesiology are creating new, indigenous training programs for pastors and lay leaders. They are forming learning communities of pastors and lay leaders and creating networks of support to encourage experimentation and to help manage change. Grassroots funding streams and indigenous church planting models are being developed without reliance on national church money or direction. Expertise is being brought in from outside denominational structures. These judicatories are not waiting for someone else to provide leadership.

The locus of energy in the church has shifted downward, providing an opportunity for national church structures to reshape their ministry in service to these "bottom-up" initiatives.

An Opportunity to Empower Discipleship

Missional theology radicalizes the Reformation concept of the priesthood of all believers. The missional church movement seeks to break down the distance between ordained clergy and laypeople in following Christ into the twenty-first-century mission field. The professionalization of the ministry, following the lead of major secular professions like law and medicine, has created an unhealthy and unfaithful distance between clergy and laypeople. It also encourages passivity about discipleship as a way of life among all believers as opposed to "church membership," which is a once-a-week activity supported by the credentialed church professionals.

The Church of England is actively experimenting with equipping and empowering laypeople to plant congregations and to lead revitalization efforts in dying congregations, with pastors providing the ministry of Word and Sacrament as a part of these initiatives.

Missional thinking also encourages disciples to see their ministry not in terms of service to the church, but in terms of being sent into the world. One's work life, family life, recreational life, and community life all become the focus of discipleship and redefine the meaning and boundaries of "church."

An Opportunity to Reclaim the Apostolic Vocation

"Why doesn't the Presbyterian Church have apostles?" This question was posed to me by several Pentecostal pastors who were a part of my small group for five days at the Missional Leadership Conference in England I attended last summer. In their view, "apostles" referred to future-oriented, visionary leaders who were always "seeing" new ministry opportunities in the mission field. No church should be without its apostles, they argued. In fact, you couldn't have a church without them. Their denomination (The Apostolic Church in the UK) systematically identifies congregants with apostolic gifts and integrates these "apostles" into local church ministry teams.

The missional church is apostolic in the sense that "church" is never limited to "the members" or "the building" but looks beyond itself to embrace the whole community in participating in God's mission in the world.

One deficiency in our contemporary definition of the pastoral role is that it typically does not include a self-conscious understanding of the apostolic vocation. So where are the apostles of our own day? Perhaps we need to start looking for people in our pews who have apostolic sensibilities and start to nurture and utilize their gifts to complement the traditional pastoral role.

An Opportunity for Prophetic Witness

In the United States, historically, Christian churches have been under enormous social pressure to conform to the values, moral codes, and general lifestyle approved by the policy-making majority. As practiced in the United States, Christendom not only limited the extent of the churches' freedom *from* society; it also greatly impeded the church's freedom *for* society. This was the point with which Reinhold Niebuhr began his book *The Interpretation of Christian Ethics*, as shown in its remarkable opening sentence: "Protestant Christianity in America is, unfortunately, unduly dependent upon the very culture of modernity, the disintegration of which would offer a more independent religion a unique opportunity."

The freedom that accompanies disestablishment is not for the purpose of becoming a self-serving enclave divorced from the world. It is, rather, the necessary condition for the exercise of social and worldly responsibility. We can only be in the world as disciples of Christ if we are not simply of the world but also find the source of our life beyond the world's own ways and possibilities.

Since U.S. churches have been so reluctant to pursue a course distinct from their host culture, their present rejection by that culture may be the Spirit's way of ensuring a sufficient distance from the world to enable the churches to be of some worldly use by serving as instruments of our missionary God. Rather than fearing our disestablishment, we are being invited to participate in it actively by reclaiming our prophetic vocation.

An Opportunity Not to Waste This Crisis

I believe this is the most exciting and hopeful time to be a Christian in the United States. The sea change that is now in process gives us the opportunity to return to our missional roots. The ministry of Clifton Kirkpatrick has, in many ways, provided us a vision for this work. It is now up to us, under the guidance of the Holy Spirit, not to let this crisis go to waste.

Chapter 3

The Joy of Growing Old

At times in our lifetime we may wonder: When I grow old, . . . will I live, or just survive?

But in fact, when does old age start? It starts with the beginning of life itself. There is no such thing as "school age" or "active life age." You can be active until your death. Life is indivisible. And this indivisibility of life is just at the core of human existence. The night rounds off the day. The morning is beautiful, as well as the afternoon, but the most beautiful thing is the very existence of morning, afternoon, evening, and night. That's why I am so moved by the Brazilian poet and theologian Rubem Alves's words: "I want to have a long life but not at any price. I want to live as long as I have the ability to be moved by beauty and the name for that emotion before beauty is 'joy.'"[1] That means that living a full life is not only a biological issue—a heartbeat or an electric brain wave. When joy ceases, the body becomes a coffin, no matter the age of that body. Thus human life is not only a product of nature. It also exists and continues to exist as long as we have the ability to experience beauty and happiness.

New Ways to Begin Our Lives

Two Cuban witnesses have confirmed my paradigm for living the beginning of this period of seniority in hope and dignity. I have called these two witnesses "new ways to begin our lives."

Translated from the Spanish by the editor; thanks are also due to Mrs. Elizabeth Quintero-Ramos, staff at the Presbytery of Elizabeth, who assisted the editor in refining the translation.

On his fiftieth birthday, Rafael Cepeda wrote that he was beginning to live. At sixty he decided to devote himself to a great dream: "writing and rediscovering the history of his church." He produced the research about the "Patriotic Missionaries," which even changed the anniversary dates of some of our churches. By rereading and rewriting this history, he gave his time and his sagacity as a researcher and writer by opening up new avenues to understanding the Cuban Church.

The second witness comes from René Castellanos Morente. At the age of seventy, he was working in Nicaragua in a theological training project for church leaders. I was working at the World Council of Churches in Geneva when I received a letter from him, asking for help to buy an Arabic-Spanish Dictionary. "I have started studying Arabic, and I need that book," he said.

I purchased the book and sent it to him in Nicaragua. By this I mean that each moment of our life may imply new life projects.

Open Doors That No One Can Close

Consequently, the figure of Cliff Kirkpatrick as he reaches the age of seventy inspires me to say that I can see, touch, identify, and appreciate his "joy for growing old" in the continuation of his life, and that moves me profoundly.

Now, being careful not to fall into any fragmentation or atomization of his life, I am going to refer to Cliff as the man who has lived the gospel in a prophetic-apocalyptic manner, inspired in the essence of the last book of the Bible, which is the book of hope, of human hope, of Christian hope, of divine hope. Based on this book, I am going to apply the passage of the community of Philadelphia (Rev. 3:7–13). In spite of having no economic, political, social, or institutional power, this community was praised for its faithfulness to Jesus' project, as shown in keeping his word and fearlessly opposing those of the "synagogue of Satan." I do not see this text as anti-Semitic but as referring to the false Jews and hypocritical Pharisees who submissively praised the empire.

In my opinion the passage that best describes Cliff Kirkpatrick's position as a churchman comes from Revelation, as it speaks to a community: "I know your works. Look, I have set before you an open door, which no one is able to shut. I know that you have but little power, and yet you have kept my word and have not denied my name" (Rev. 3:8).

The expression "an open door" or "to open a door" is often used in the New Testament as well as in the Old Testament. Isaiah 22:22 says, "I will place on his shoulder the key of the house of David; he shall open, and no one shall shut; he shall shut, and no one shall open."

The apostle Paul uses the metaphor of "an open door" in Corinthians and Colossians as opportunities for mission. And this has been Cliff's essential characteristic. He has been able to open doors that nobody has been able to close. The Cuban Church acknowledges the formidable quality of this American leader who worked so hard as an ecclesiastical leader of a U.S. church to break the barriers separating our two countries. He opened doors and managed to put an end to the isolation to which we were being submitted, by crossing frontiers from church to church, and by supporting new initiatives that sought to break barriers with unflinching energy.

The World Alliance of Reformed Churches also found his support for the Accra Confession approved by its General Council in Ghana in 2004, in defense of the countries that are facing discrimination, oppression, and exclusion; today this confession serves as a permanent inspiration for our churches in the global South. That open door in Accra, Ghana, cannot be closed either; it was an extraordinary step in our Reformed tradition to open new paths for the transformation of our societies and churches.

From Cliff Kirkpatrick, we have learned the willingness of looking in-depth toward the future; it is this willingness that promotes hope and gives meaning to prophetic action.

Judith's beautiful prayer gives content to this prophetic action: "But you are the God of the lowly, helper of the oppressed, upholder of the weak, protector of the forsaken, savior of those without hope" (9:11).

The Power of Wisdom

Elisabeth Schüssler Fiorenza invites us to "dance along the roads of wisdom," for which "having dancing shoes is not enough. It also requires energy and determination. The struggle for justice also calls for devotion and strength. Looking closely at the Bible in search of the power coming from Wisdom is one of the forms of strengthening our spirit and of keeping our commitment alive."[2]

The main characteristic of the "spirit of wisdom" in the Bible is the action that helps us to lead our lives creatively, above all, maintaining the passion for justice as the hermeneutical element in the mission of God.

There are at least three chief elements in the biblical power of wisdom that are present in Cliff Kirkpatrick's life and work:

1. The biblical tradition of wisdom always guides Christology beyond humankind, toward the ecology of the Earth and of the universe.
2. The content of wisdom always leads us toward a global ecumenical perspective that includes other religions.
3. God's passion, shown in the incarnation and suffering of wisdom in Jesus Christ, guides us to the search for justice and peace. God's passion always searches for the eradication of oppression and the establishment of just relations.[3]

According to Sharon H. Ringe, three texts in the Hebrew Bible introduce the term "wisdom" to show the identification of creation in conformity with the will of God and with the nature of the Creator.[4] Psalm 104; Job 28; and Proverbs 1–9 are among the passages of great significance that speak to the mysteries of biblical wisdom:

> O LORD, how manifold are your works!
>   In wisdom you have made them all;
>   the earth is full of your creatures.
>   (Ps. 104:24)

In Western thought, people are prone to consider Earth, with its roots, seas, and sands, as inanimate. Human beings are living subjects, while Earth is an inanimate object. However, in the text we are studying, the earth is a living thing, a subject that can be healed.

If we have to cooperate with the Spirit/Wisdom in the cleaning up of our personal life, there is no doubt that we should cooperate with that same Spirit in the cleaning up of Earth, where we were born.

The Spirit/Wisdom becomes a public presence with important claims in the book of Proverbs.

> Wisdom cries out in the street;
>   in the squares she raises her voice.
> At the busiest corner she cries out;
>   at the entrance of the city gates she speaks.
>   (1:20–21)

> Does not wisdom call,
>   and does not understanding raise her voice?
> On the heights, beside the way,
>   at the crossroads she takes her stand;
> besides the gates in front of the town,
>   at the entrance of the portals she cries out.
>   (8:1–3)

The message that she brings is

- *Truth*: "For my mouth will utter truth." (8:7)
- *Knowledge*: "rather than choice gold." (8:10b)
- *Justice*: "I walk in the way of righteousness, along the paths of justice." (8:20)
- *Life*: "For whoever finds me finds life and obtains favor from the LORD." (8:35) "She [instruction] is your life." (4:13)

These four elements are central in Cliff Kirkpatrick's life and work.

Spirit—Wisdom in Action

This is an invitation to carry out a wisdom movement for the justice and well-being of all. Following the guidance of wisdom, our first statement for action must be the search for truth.

So our question is "To what extent can we really consider the church to be a truth zone?" Do our way of doing theology, our church policies, and our faith practice conform an authentic "truth zone"?

The Hebrew term *'emet* means not only truth but also truthfulness, which is nothing else than an ethical requirement. It implies sincerity, honesty, and authenticity. The path of truth means giving up egotism and following Jesus' path. It is what Ivone Gebara has called "a Christic life" and Juan Stam calls "a eucharistic life."

We need to transform our local churches, our church organizations, our governments and societies, our daily life into zones of truthfulness where Christ's message of grace, truth, and life leads our very existence, our world, and our living together with God and with our neighbors.

The second wisdom element necessary for mission is knowing and sharing our wisdom, information, and scientific discoveries. Everything that helps to sustain and maintain life is basic for the achievement of justice. In the midst of the contemporary economic crisis, where hunger is gaining more and more space in people's life, the message of divine Wisdom brings us closer to a life of sharing our daily bread with those who lack it. Let's hear her voice:

> Wisdom bought a house and set the table;
> Told the servants to go and cried to the people:
> "Come and share my bread, drink the wine I have made for you."
> Wisdom, a worker for justice whose banners are knowledge and life,
> And whose messengers are the prophets and poets,
> Is announcing the *ekklēsia* seated at Its table.[5]

The invitation of divine Wisdom to bread, well-being, beauty, and knowledge gives us rich opportunities for the full enjoyment of a new beginning in any stage of our life.

Conclusion: Some Advice for More and Better Living

To live well, it is necessary to accept life as a succession of challenges, and the challenges, indeed, are a way to live and enjoy life more.

Moreover, life is beautiful and full of details that make life deserving of that enjoyment: the smile of a little boy or a little girl, the glance of a woman, a flower or sensing the smell of one, the hand that holds us when we fall, the one who is sincerely moved in the presence of our sorrow, the enjoyment of a book or a work of art, even the satisfaction from a job well done—these are some of the millions of phenomena that we encounter daily and make life an invaluable gift that we must enjoy and desire to prolong.

That capacity of feeling joy in the presence of small actions in our daily lives is the essence of life. But above all, we should not limit ourselves, nor should we let others limit us. As we grow older, we tend to limit ourselves from some things. Our relatives and the people who surround us contribute in setting more limitations, sometimes even when their love tries to protect us. To avoid our self-limitation and the limitations that others try to impose on us, the most important thing is motivation.

Motivation is the basic part in life. Anything can motivate us: helping in the education of those surrounding us, in the family, in the seminaries, in the church; devoting ourselves to realizing some artistic activities; cultivating a garden; organizing groups of friends—just to mention a few things.

In summary, to make yourself feel useful, use all of your experiences that you have accumulated your whole life.

If we are trying to live and not simply trying to survive, then the twilight of our existence can become a rich, luminous, and irreplaceable part of life.

Chapter 4

Rediscovering *Missio Dei*

A Challenge to the Churches

HIS HOLINESS ARAM I, CATHOLICOS OF CILICIA

*M*arch 2009, Antelias, Lebanon

The ecumenical movement has reminded the churches that they do not have a *missio ecclesiae*, a mission of their own; instead, they are called to share in the *missio Dei*. With its multitude of crises, the world of today has sharpened the crucial urgency of this reminder. In their attempt to rediscover the *missio Dei*, the churches are challenged to identify its imperatives and implications in the context of the globalized world.

From Functional to Essential Perception of Mission

Mission is the *esse* of the church, not its function. The church is a mission-ary reality, and this basic affirmation constitutes the heart of the church's self-understanding.

For many years, in church and ecumenical circles, we used to refer to "church" and "mission" as though they were different entities. We discussed the "mission of the church," as though mission were one of the activities of the church. Even "mission agencies" were considered to be outside the institutional boundaries and conciliar structures of the church. These misper-ceptions need to be corrected. Indeed, it is through mission that the church acquires its essential nature, true meaning, and authentic vocation. We must not separate mission from church by making it a program of a specialized agency or a mere department of the church. Considering church and mission together as one inseparable whole is not a methodological or strategic ques-tion: it is an ontological necessity. Ecclesiology is essentially missiology.

Missio Dei calls the church to understand itself as a mission. It also calls us to develop an integrated approach to church and mission. Rediscovering the *missio Dei* as the raison d'être of the church is a major priority facing the church in the twenty-first century.

From *Missio Ecclesiae* back to *Missio Dei*

The church does not exist for itself; it exists for a mission entrusted to it by God in Christ. The church is sent into the world; its mandate is taking Christ to the world and announcing the restoration of the kingdom of God. Therefore, there is no so-called *missio ecclesiae* but only *missio Dei*. Church-centered mission contradicts the church's very being. It distorts the specific nature and purpose of God's mission and makes the church a self-contained and a self-sufficient reality, exclusively concerned with its self-perpetuation.

Historical circumstances, including political, cultural, and ethnic considerations, have had a strong impact on the churches' missionary understanding and practice. For some churches, mission has been considered mainly as the church going out; for others, emphasis is placed on increase in membership and even proselytism. *Missio Dei* liberates the church from institutionalism and builds up *koinōnia*. It transforms the inward looking of the church into a creative interaction of the church with its environment. It ensures the quality of the church's life and its dynamic engagement in society. *Missio ecclesiae* must derive its authenticity from *missio Dei* and must be accountable to it.

Missio Dei Is Catholic

In its nature, scope, and purpose, *missio Dei* is catholic. It is the catholic act of the catholic church. Through the church's missionary act, the local church's inner catholicity, as a God-given vocation, acquires its fullness and concrete manifestation. *Missio Dei* is both the global action of the local church and the local action of the global church. *Missio Dei* challenges parochialism and builds up the church of a given place. It challenges confessionalism and promotes inculturation and contextualization. Indeed, the credibility of the church's missionary outreach is tested by its missionary inreach at home, on the local level. Although God's purpose is universal, *missio Dei* is always particular.

Missio Dei generates and sustains creative interaction between missionary inreach and outreach, the local and global. It saves the church from becoming a self-centered reality and opens it to God's salvific act in Christ. It helps the local church to transcend its geographical boundaries, ethnic and cultural confines, and creates ecclesial and conciliar interdependence between the local churches.

Missio Dei Is Holistic

In its purpose, *missio Dei* is holistic, embracing the whole of humanity and the creation. The goal of *missio Dei* is a reconciled and transformed humanity and creation. *Missio Dei* is also holistic in its action, engaging the whole church through its *kerygma, leitourgia, diakonia, martyria,* and *koinōnia.* These dimensions, manifestations, and actions of the church are directed toward the proclamation of the kingdom.

Hence, with its holistic nature and inclusive approach, *missio Dei* challenges rigid christocentrism and enhances a Trinitarian perspective. It questions "private Christianity" and calls for a *koinōnia* of faith, love, and hope. It challenges ecclesiocentric perceptions of mission and promotes *koinōnia*-centered practice of mission. *Missio Dei* provides an all-embracing vision of life, history, humanity, and creation. To avoid emerging fragmentation and disintegration in many spheres of church and society life, a renewed emphasis and articulation need to be given to *missio Dei.*

Missio Dei Is Eschatological

Missio Dei is a witness to Christ, who has come and will come again. As such, it transcends time and geography and is eschatological. History and eschaton interact; vertical and horizontal embrace each other; and the past, the present, and the future enter in dynamic dialogue in and through *missio Dei.* The Bible affirms that in Christ and with the power of the Holy Spirit, all "things in heaven and on earth" (Eph. 1:10) will be united; the whole creation and humanity will be renewed and transformed with the *parousia* (Rev. 21:5; 22:12).

Too much stress on the "historical Jesus" has often overshadowed the "eschatological Jesus." The good news of missionaries has depicted the profile of a person who has come at a given time and in a given place, almost ignoring the promise of his second coming. *Missio Dei* announces both the faith in resurrection and eschatological hope. It underscores the Christ event, and at the same time it takes Christ beyond the boundaries of geography and history. This peculiar feature of Christian faith—which ensures the spiritual vitality, the inner catholicity, and the eschatological perenniality of *koinōnia*—must permeate and underpin the church's missionary self-understanding and action in all places and times.

Missio Dei Is Prophetic

The church derives its prophetic vocation from *missio Dei*. Indeed, preaching "Christ crucified" and resurrected (1 Cor. 1:23) implies *kenōsis* and *martyria* in life, and even in death. *Missio Dei* has profound implications.

It calls for a serving church. Mission does not provide knowledge about Christ; it takes Christ as a living reality to the world by proclaiming in deed God's redeeming love, healing power, and reconciling action in Christ; it reaches to the marginalized and to the poor, not by giving bread or advice but by providing justice and calling for accountability structures that generate oppression and injustice.

Missio Dei calls for a combating church. Entrusted by God's mission, the church cannot close its ears to the cries of the voiceless; it cannot remain indifferent to a savage and uncontrolled free-market economy, which generates corruption and greed; it cannot ignore the degradation of the ecosystem, which may lead the whole creation to total destruction; and it cannot tolerate a value system that encourages anthropocentrism in all aspects of human life and generates decay of spiritual and moral values. The church must discern the will of God in today's world and respond faithfully to the imperatives of *missio Dei*.

In the midst of societies marked by consumerism, secularism, terrorism, and materialism, *missio Dei* strives for a quality of life articulated in and through Christ. It liberates communities and people from marginalization and promotes integration. It overcomes hopelessness and provides hope for the future.

Missio Dei Is a Source of Unity

To receive the good news means to be incorporated into the body of Christ. God's mission brings the local churches together in a common action for a common cause. If the churches' mission is *missio Dei*, it cannot be otherwise. As God's reconciliation with humanity in Christ (2 Cor. 5:19; Eph. 2:14), *missio Dei* ultimately aims at the unity of humanity. Unity of the church is a sign, anticipation, and foretaste of the unity of humanity. God in Christ will "gather up all things in him, things in heaven and things on earth" (Eph. 1:10).

In my view, the question "mission or unity?" raised in the ecumenical movement is a false dichotomy. The churches may have different perceptions, methodologies, or priorities in respect to mission. They may have different ecclesiological self-understanding, which may impact their approach to mission. But these differences must not lead to conflict. Instead of becoming the agents of *missio Dei*, the missionaries have often pursued the interests of colonial powers. In many regions the parochial and confessional approach to mission and competitive missionary activities have created new divisions. *Missio Dei* unites the churches, while *missio ecclesiae* divides them. *Missio Dei* deepens the God-given unity of the church by giving tangible expression to the ecclesial interdependence existing between the local churches; *missio ecclesiae* creates disintegration and leads the church to self-isolation. Indeed, within the framework of *missio Dei*, the churches' ecclesiological, doctrinal, and theological differences are transformed into reconciled diversities.

No Compromise on *Missio Dei*

Mission is not a question of choice; it belongs to God. Mission is given as a sacred commandment to each Christian: "You will be my witnesses . . . to the ends of the earth" (Acts 1:8; Matt. 28:19–20; Mark 16:15). Under any circumstances, therefore, God's mission cannot be compromised. *Martyria* is precisely that action of a church or a Christian by which any withdrawal from mission is rejected to the extent of shedding blood. The history of Christianity is rich with *martyria*.

The church has no right to own Christ by confining him inside the walls of the church. God's salvific purpose is universal and cosmic. In the power of the Holy Spirit, *missio Dei* empowers and sends the church "to the ends of the earth." Christ came to save the whole humanity. Hence, God's mission does not recognize limits or limitations. It must be ready to discover new frontiers and open itself to new horizons. The proclamation of the kingdom of God to the world and encountering Christ in the Other by respecting the otherness of the Other is crucial for *missio Dei*.

A pluralist society is both a challenge and a risk for mission. The church cannot sacrifice *missio Dei* on the altar of interreligious dialogue. *Missio Dei* must avoid a crusading spirit and proselytizing approaches. An excessive christocentric approach to mission may also hinder *missio Dei*. I believe that a *diakonia* of love and ministry of healing and reconciliation can ensure a solid basis and credible paradigm for the church's missionary engagement.

Chapter 5

Funding and Faithfulness

The Political Economy of Christian Mission

PHILIP L. WICKERI

As director of the Worldwide Ministries Division of the Presbyterian Church (U.S.A.), as PC(USA) stated clerk, and as president of the World Alliance of Reformed Churches, Clifton Kirkpatrick has combined a passion for global mission, ecumenism, and the prophetic witness of the church. In this essay, my intention is to bring these concerns together by considering the crisis we are now experiencing in the ecumenical mission of our churches. This crisis is often spoken of in terms of funding, but I suggest that it is much deeper than that. How churches use and attract economic resources for mission and ecumenism (what the church does in its life and witness) is related to the very basis of Christian faith (who the church is in faithfulness to Jesus Christ). I call this the political economy of Christian mission, a term we have not often used in discussions of the *missio Dei*.

The political economy of mission is important because it is increasingly evident that our current financial crisis is having a direct impact on church institutions. This is especially evident in church and mission programs in the global South and has been so for some time. But even in the North, churches have begun to directly experience the effects of the global financial crisis. At the seminary where I teach, we have begun a series of dramatic economic cutbacks that are informed more by a certain perception of economic realities and sociological trends than by a creative vision for the future. Similarly, the downsizing of denominations—including but not limited to the PC(USA)— and ecumenical organizations has been dictated by management theories that take precedence over theological convictions. Church institutions do not derive their vision and mission from worldly trends and institutional theories but from faithfulness to Jesus Christ. For this reason we need a perspective

24

on the political economy of Christian mission to help us uncover what we are now involved in and recover our faithfulness to Jesus Christ.

In the present situation, I found the words of Rowan Williams, Archbishop of Canterbury, both candid and refreshing. He identifies the myths and fictions that lie behind our economic situation and are at the root of our current crisis:

> Marx long ago observed the way in which unbridled capitalism became a kind of mythology, ascribing reality, power, and agency to things that had no life in themselves; he was right about that, if about little else. . . . This crisis exposes the element of basic unreality in the situation—the truth that almost unimaginable wealth has been generated by equally unimaginable levels of fiction, paper transactions with no concrete outcome beyond profit for traders. . . . Given that the risk to social stability overall in these processes has been shown to be so enormous, it is no use pretending that the financial world can maintain indefinitely the degree of exemption from scrutiny and regulation that it has got used to.[1]

Williams's comments in the fall 2008 came as world leaders were gathering in New York for the UN General Assembly discussions of the Millennium Development Goals. Other church and ecumenical leaders have said that the financial crisis must not be used as an excuse to curtail global anti-poverty plans. Mainline churches and the ecumenical movement have had a noble history of speaking prophetically about economic issues. I am particularly thinking of the Accra Confession (2004) of WARC and the AGAPE process of the World Council of Churches. This, however, is not my subject. Instead, I want to internalize the discussion of economic issues as they affect the life and work of churches themselves.

The ways in which we organize our economic life for mission are related to who we are as Christians. Yet this is a subject that no church, no ecumenical body, no theological institution has dared to speak to or address. In conversations I have had with church and ecumenical leaders over the past several years, I have been told that it is a subject they could not address, whether out of fear of undercutting their own economic base, offending donors, or appearing to be self-interested in questions of their own survival. We surely are part of the very economy that we make statements about. But when it comes to our own finances, churches tend to shy away from asking fundamental questions about how we use our resources and how financial interests outside the church shape church activities.

The subject of political economy originated in moral philosophy with the work of Adam Smith (1723–90). In other words, it started as a theological and ethical question. Since Smith's writing in the late eighteenth century, the subject of political economy has been developed in a variety of different ways that cannot concern us here. What does concern us is the task for a political economy of Christian mission: to investigate and question the patterns of church support and the funding of mission and ecumenism in order to disclose the underlying sociological and political premises of partnership, ecumenism, and mission sharing.[2] In other words, from the perspective of the political economy of mission, our theological constructs *about* the *missio Dei* are not in themselves the basic frameworks for analysis. Rather, our theologies of mission are themselves expressions of beliefs and actions that must be explained and interpreted in terms that are more than theological. This should be self-evident to any Calvinist, but churches have deliberately avoided questioning the processes involved in our own financial decision making. We like to receive money, but we do not like to talk about what is involved in getting it. The subject makes us uncomfortable because it is so "secular."

The political economy of mission is interwoven with the political economy of the global systems of which we are a part. Although there have been different ideologies of political economy (neoliberal, nationalist, Marxist-Leninist), the global economic system that emerged in the late 1970s was dominated by neoliberalism and American-led interests and institutions.[3] This was even more the case after the fall of the Soviet Union in 1989. The economic ideology may be changing in light of our current crisis, but we can say that the changes in the global economy that began in the late 1970s were reflected in the political economy of mission. More to the point, what I would call "Christian Capital" emerged as a significant economic force in the churches over the last thirty years, particularly in the United States, with a premise and an ethos that closely resembled neoliberal globalization. To turn Max Weber around, this was a capitalist ethic in the spirit of Protestantism.

The questions we have to ask are basic: how does funding, the absence of funding, or the ready availability of funding shape the church and its mission programs? What does this mean in terms of mission accountability, unequal access to economic resources, and the use of economic power in churches in the North and the South? These questions are related to theological understandings of "stewardship," but the issues are broader, different, and more basic. Stewardship questions revolve around the resources that we have; funding questions are concerned with resources we do not necessarily have, or resources we can have if we do certain things. Contributions and donations to the work of the church do not just come; they have to be sought. And in the seeking, there is always an interactive process between the donor (patron?) and the recipient (client?) involving factors that are more than theological.

Funding has always been an issue for Christian faithfulness in mission. The modern Protestant missionary movement was initially funded by trading and shipping interests, and through the tithes, contributions, and donations of devout laymen and laywomen. There has thus far been too little study of the funding of the nineteenth- and twentieth-century mission movements, or of church funding today. It would be an unjust exaggeration to say that Protestant mission has been *determined* by the patterns of funding, but it is also naive to think that the availability of money and material resources is *irrelevant* to how we spread the gospel.

What is now needed is a deeper discussion of the political economy of mission, a subject that has been taboo in churches and ecumenical organizations. This need is evident when we consider, as an example, the word "partnership."[4] It seems that almost everyone is "partnering" in mission with someone these days. "Mission is from everywhere to everywhere," many Presbyterians like to say, and mission always involves partnership. However, some forms of partnerships are more like leveraged buyouts, insofar as there are implicit and explicit elements of control. Who decides what partnership is? How are the terms of a given partnership agreed upon? A wealthy Presbyterian church in Southern California works with its "own denomination" in Africa. South Korean Presbyterians start a seminary in St. Petersburg for the churches they have established. These and other initiatives need to be analyzed by using political-economic as well as theological categories. The term "partnership in mission" used to mean that we were engaged in an exchange between churches and among different expressions of the worldwide body of Christ. This is still the proper theological use of the term. However, many of today's "partnering" arrangements may more accurately be described as economic exchanges, often with the best of intentions, but a far cry from churches walking together in mission.

In this short essay, I have only been able to raise questions, not offer solutions. But the premise of these questions is my belief that we are accountable to the people we serve and to God in Christ who is Lord of all. We are called to remain true to the *missio Dei* even as we seek to envision a future that we cannot clearly see. Our mission must drive our efforts in funding and fund-raising, not the other way around. We cannot and must not allow the availability or absence of funds to determine what we can and cannot do. That would mean selling the gospel to the highest bidder and entering a neoliberal free market of missions. We confess that we are shaped by our political economy, but we cannot allow our churches to be held captive to it. The challenge this poses for Presbyterian and Reformed churches is that we seek to live out the Accra Confession as it applies to our life together in mission.

Chapter 6

With All of Our Mind

The Mission of Theological Education
in the Reformed Tradition

CYNTHIA M. CAMPBELL

*O*ne of the most prominent legacies of Presbyterian mission is education. Wherever Reformed Christians went, they founded schools, colleges, and theological seminaries. From St. Andrews to Seoul, from Cairo to Chicago, from Toronto to Princeton, from Grand Rapids to Havana—all over the world, theological colleges and seminaries prepare women and men for ministry and help the church meet the needs of changing times. Although most schools were founded to meet the needs of their particular church family, most Reformed seminaries today serve the broader church and are part of ecumenical consortia or at least have relationships with schools from other traditions.

One of the purposes of a theological school is to teach the religious tradition of the church that founded it. Indeed, a seminary is a critical part of the "traditioning" process in which faith is handed on from one generation to another and in which the tradition itself is challenged and grows through rigorous scholarship and engagement with the church. Reformed Christianity has long stressed the importance of theological ideas. Extended debate about the sovereignty of God, the importance of Scripture, and the nature of Christ's saving work has shaped not only Reformed life but the broader Christian church as well.

Without in any way diminishing the importance of such scholarship, I argue that education in Reformed theological schools does more than teach a system of doctrine. Theological education in the Reformed tradition demonstrates a way of approaching Christian faith. At its best, it enables people to engage Christian faith according to four theological "habits of the heart": *appreciation*, *suspicion*, *engagement*, and *gratitude*.

Appreciation

On our better days, Reformed Christians have gratefully acknowledged that we are not "the one true church" and that Reformed Christians are not the only ones who are saved. Notwithstanding some rather exclusive tendencies down through the years, there is at least in principle an openness to the breadth of the Christian experience of others, which I would call an *appreciation* of the gifts of other parts of the tradition.

This is evident, first of all, in the importance of studying the history of the church and the history of biblical interpretation. Calvin himself is an excellent example of this. His use of the theologians of the early church helped the reforming church to recognize that there was great value from the past that could be brought forward as the church sought to be faithful in a new day. Like Calvin, we today expect to find insight and wisdom from those who have gone before us and to make those resources available to the church at large.

Appreciation for the life and work of other Christians is not only a matter of understanding and making use of the past. It also involves recognition of the importance of the life experience of the church in different cultures. As Christianity has become a part of cultures around the world, insights into Scripture have emerged that continue to broaden our understanding of the faith and reshape theological ideas. In the 1960s, Christians in Latin America and then other regions began to see their own struggles against poverty and political oppression through the lens of biblical stories such as the exodus. More recently, theologians and biblical scholars have reflected on the ways Jesus and early Christians related to the Roman Empire and the significance this has for a postcolonial understanding of world Christianity.

Finally, Reformed Christians recognize that God is at work everywhere, not just in the church and among believers. Because the whole universe is God's realm, we are convinced that Christian faith can learn from other fields of human inquiry: from the sciences, the humanities, and from other faith traditions. The motto of the campus ministry program at Presbyterian-related Austin College put it this way: "God gave us minds and expects us to use them." Because God is the creator of the whole universe and of the human mind and intellect, Christian faith has nothing to fear from scientific exploration or artistic expression.

Suspicion

The Reformed tradition has long held that every aspect of human life is marred by sin and that every culture has built-in blind spots. Because the church is a human institution as well as the body of Christ, we assert that there is no such thing as a perfect church. The Reformation-era confessions declare that the church has from time to time "erred": it has been mistaken in both belief and practice and therefore must continually be reformed.

Such a theological foundation leads to education that values critical thinking and assumes that theological, political, and economic ideas will always be subject to limitations and therefore must be subjected to regular review and critique. This way of educating can be unsettling both for teachers and learners. We all become comfortable with what we have learned and with what has always "worked" for us theologically. But the Reformed tradition reminds us that we can make an idol out of anything, even good theological ideas.

Engagement

One feature of the Reformed emphasis on God's sovereignty is the conviction that there is no aspect of human life about which God is not concerned. Business, politics, home and family life, science and technology, the performing and visual arts, social organization and relationships—all of these are part of the religious life because they are part of the world that God loves. Likewise, a Reformed theological education encourages teachers and students to engage the issues of the everyday world and wonder what God is doing in and through human life and culture. It teaches students how to read context as well as text, to discern the distinctive character of particular social locations and the impact those locations have on the interpretation of texts.

In addition, a Reformed education leads to a practice of ministry that is similarly engaged with the world. As the United Presbyterian Church of North America wrote in the early twentieth century, one of the "great ends" of the church is "the promotion of social righteousness." As Reformed people read the Bible, God desires societies as well as individuals to practice justice, to show compassion, and to care for the poor. Thus, a vision of ministry that engages in social witness and works for transformation in social institutions is found in many Reformed theological schools.

Gratitude

To borrow the phrase from contemporary American theologian Brian Gerrish, the gospel and our response can be summed up in the phrase "grace and gratitude." The good news is that God comes to us first and last in love freely and unconditionally given in Jesus Christ. We do not deserve it; we cannot earn it. All we can do is receive it with grateful hearts and generous lives. A corollary is that the Christian life is *not* about fear. When the Bible says that the "fear of the LORD is the beginning of wisdom" (Prov. 9:10), it means having respect or awe for God. It does not mean fear in the sense of "We don't know what God might do next"—because we *do* know. God will always be faithful to God's promises and to the covenant God has made with all humankind. God will never be other than the way we see God in the life, ministry, death, and resurrection of Jesus Christ.

This way of approaching God and the life of faith is the ultimate liberation. Life that is grounded in gratitude is hopeful, confident, and generous. It enables individuals and congregations, denominations and theological schools to embrace new experiences and take risks confident of God's promise never to leave us on our own. It encourages exploration of new ideas even if they challenge long-held ideas or practices. It makes it possible to witness to the saving love of Jesus Christ while also affirming the dignity and worth of people from all cultures and traditions as beloved children of one God.

Reformed Christians are doing faithful work in theological schools around the world preparing men and women for leadership in the church of Jesus Christ. Many schools do this with few resources and often face challenges from societies threatened by Reformed ways of being faithful. But when leaders of these schools gather, there is a palpable feeling of joy in the work of teaching and learning and gratitude for the opportunity to love God with all of our mind.

Chapter 7

When Mission and Justice Embrace

HUNTER FARRELL

Beginning in 1984, the world was confronted with horrendous televised images of starving children and their weeping mothers, victims of the now-infamous Ethiopian famine that eventually claimed more than one million lives. Christian churches responded generously, including Ethiopian famine relief as a mission priority. Together with a wide array of governments and nonprofit organizations, the international community quickly generated more than $100 million to provide direct food aid.

But as media attention moved elsewhere, some troubling facts began to emerge. Although the humanitarian crisis had been framed as a famine, throughout the 1980s there actually was enough food produced in Ethiopia to feed its entire population. But in the national context of the rebellion of the Tigray, Eritrea, and Wollo regions against the brutal Derg regime in Addis Ababa, the root problem was one of food distribution: the government, after engineering widespread starvation to punish the rebels, adeptly diverted the donated food aid from the needy to feed its own army. The end result was chilling: "The humanitarian effort prolonged the war and, with it, human suffering," concluded renowned British researcher Alex de Waal after his exhaustive study of the international response to the famine.[1] Because well-intended Christian mission efforts had ignored the underlying structural injustices, well-intended help was misdirected, and tens of thousands more Ethiopians died. Mission without justice ceased to be God's mission at all.

In our globalizing world, recent trends in the way the Presbyterian Church (U.S.A.) engages in international mission have led to the marginalization of a focus on justice in mission activities. This case study will briefly reflect on the historic relationship of justice and mission, assess the impact of recent trends, and examine a new model of doing mission with justice.

Historical Foundations

The mission history of the Reformed churches bears witness to the integral relationship of justice and mission. Calvin taught this holistic understanding of God's mission, advocating for the just distribution of society's goods and for the responsible care of God's creation, and preaching and writing against slavery.[2] Despite the polarization that later resulted in the U.S. churches from the social gospel debate,[3] historically, alongside preaching, teaching, and healing, many nineteenth- and twentieth-century Presbyterian mission workers found themselves drawn into the struggles of the people they were called to serve. Because of their understanding of Christ's mission, some mission workers advocated against the East Asian practices of foot-binding and female child abandonment; others worked against the scandalous abuses committed against Congolese villagers by Belgian King Leopold's rubber barons in the Congo Free State, or against the violence of the U.S. government's undeclared wars in Central America in the 1980s. Partly as a result, numerous Reformed churches around the world understand justice to be foundational to God's mission, such as the Independent Presbyterian Church of Brazil's concept of *"missão integral,"* the Ethiopian Evangelical Church Mekane Yesus's "holistic mission" emphasis, the PC(USA)'s "Social Creed for the 21st Century," and WARC's Accra Confession.

Perhaps even more significantly, since the mid-1970s, the witness of the Reformed and other churches has helped to open the door to broader acceptance of the place of justice in God's mission: a growing number of parachurch ministries such as World Vision and Habitat for Humanity, after years of responding to poverty's symptoms, have developed advocacy programs to begin to address its causes. Newer ministries like the International Justice Mission motivate evangelical Christians to engage in issues of justice, while traditionally more conservative institutions such as the National Association of Evangelicals have strongly increased their public role in the debate on environmental justice and include public policy advocacy in their understanding of Christian discipleship. Thus, what David Bosch has called "the convergence of convictions" appears to be restoring justice to a more prominent place in mission as practiced by several U.S. churches and parachurch mission groups.

The Ebb of Justice in Current Missiological Practice:
A Case Study

Even so, there are several emerging cultural and missiological trends that threaten to diminish the churches' inclusion of justice as an intrinsic part of their engagement with God's mission. Since the middle of the twentieth century, a major paradigm shift has occurred in the area of international mission funding and personnel sending. In the case of the Presbyterian Church (U.S.A.), Dawson notes that, whereas in 1976, only 20 percent of the funds PC(USA) congregations sent for mission work beyond their congregations went to non-Presbyterian organizations, by 2003 that figure had risen to more than 53 percent.[4] The precipitous drop in denominational mission funding (undesignated mission funding dropped 44 percent in the ten-year period ending in 2003) led to a rapid decrease in the number of long-term mission workers sent out by the denomination—from 458 full-time international mission workers to 250 in the same period.[5] While the number of denominationally supported long-term mission workers decreased, hundreds of thousands of U.S. Presbyterians began to participate in short-term mission (STM) trips overseas.

We can deduce several results from these trends in the ways PC(USA) members engage in mission. First, the shift in support to nondenominational, parachurch missions, which are historically less focused on addressing justice issues than their denominational counterparts, suggests a lessening in the Presbyterians' commitment to the justice component of God's mission.

Second, the shift from long-term to short-term mission personnel—from the model of a career missionary working for decades with a particular people group in their particular linguistic and cultural context to that of STM groups, which often travel to a given community only once for seven to twenty days—has resulted in a reduced time frame of cross-cultural relationship. This radically reduced interface decreases the depth of analysis of local problems done by missioners, since by its very nature STM is limited to addressing immediately accessible surface symptoms, rather than the more complex root causes of a host community's problems. Moreover, the profound solidarity that often characterizes long-term mission workers' relationship with the host community—and frequently leads to advocacy—appears more difficult to develop in the STM experience, due to the reduced time frame and lack of linguistic and cultural understanding.

Finally, the movement is from a centralized, denominational mission-funding and mission-sending structure committed to *partnership*[6] with the national denominational offices of sister churches to a decentralized, less structured movement working in·*partnerships* consisting primarily of projects that link U.S. congregations with overseas congregations, institutions, or ministries. This new scene generally entails a "project focus," emphasizing funding and measurable results—a focus that can easily shift the emphasis away from the underlying issues of structural injustice and limit interventions to orphan sponsorship, house construction, or direct medical care, with more immediate but superficial results.

Joining Hands: A New Model of Mission Built on Justice

Since 2000, the PC(USA)'s Hunger Program has been involved in an innovative effort to bring together local congregations' passion for international mission with the concerns for justice to address the root causes of hunger. Nine PC(USA) presbyteries are paired with networks of churches, NGOs, and grassroots community groups in other countries; as an example, the Presbytery of Giddings-Lovejoy (92 Presbyterian congregations in Missouri and Illinois) is paired with thirteen Peruvian Protestant denominations and NGOs. Together, this network has identified some of the causes of poverty and injustice in Peru: trade and environmental justice and human rights.

Because of Peru's dependence on mining, it is particularly vulnerable to the conditions imposed on it by foreign mining companies. Under pressure from the IMF, Peru privatized a large, multimetal smelter located in the city of La Oroya, selling it for a reduced price to the Doe Run Company of St. Louis, Missouri, which agreed to clean up the smelter's air and water pollution within ten years. After twelve years, studies have concluded that Doe Run has actually increased pollution, with 97 percent of the city's children under age six suffering from lead poisoning, caused primarily by the metal smelter.[7] When local voices were silenced, a group of local mothers asked the Joining Hands Network to help. The network brought local advocates— the local Catholic parish, archdiocese, and several NGOs—together with the Lima-based Council of Protestant Churches, Peruvian faith-based and environmental NGOs, and Presbyterian congregations and the Jesuits and Dominicans in Missouri and Illinois.[8] After a period of accompaniment and analysis, the Joining Hands Network leveraged the knowledge of its local partners and the power of its U.S. partners to engage St. Louis University and the U.S. Centers for Disease Control to provide an objective evaluation of community health at virtually no cost. The study's disturbing results catapulted the community's plight into the headlines of more than five hundred U.S. newspapers, CBS News, National Public Radio, and *Christianity Today* magazine. As the conflict continues, this model of mission built on the "globalization of justice" continues to produce powerful fruits, in keeping with the best of the Reformed mission tradition, a tradition in which mission and justice embrace.

Chapter 8

Silence in Heaven for About Half an Hour

The Eschatological Dimension of Mission

DOUWE VISSER

Silence in Heaven

One of the most exciting images in the book of Revelation is the opening of the seven seals by the lamb. Chapter 6 has six seals being opened. The tension is being built up for the seventh seal. The reader has to wait and read a chapter in between because only in chapter 8 will the final seal be opened. But there is a sort of a cliff-hanger: "When the lamb opened the seventh seal, there was silence in heaven for about half an hour" (Rev. 8:1). There is an abundance of exegetical commentary about the meaning of this "silence in heaven for about half an hour." It is of no relevance for this essay to go into detail about the possible meanings. Most essential is the aspect of tension that goes with this period of waiting. We could see this period of waiting in heaven as in contrast with a time of action on earth. Action here on earth has the eschatological dimension of heaven waiting before taking the final step.

The Mission of the Church in the Period of Waiting

Often, especially in more evangelical circles, mission is being embedded in feelings of eschatological tension. We have been given a short time (only "half an hour") to win as many as possible for Jesus Christ, to make sure that as many as possible are being saved on the day of the final judgment. In this sense, God's waiting is being seen as God's patience. Before he takes the final step, he is patiently waiting for us to bring in as many souls to be saved as possible. Here lies the cause of what is being called "the extreme eschatologization" of mission. The positive aspect of this is that God's waiting is not being met by passive waiting on the side of the church, as though there is no need for action. It is contradictory to the classical Reformed doctrine that the number of those to be saved has been predestined already: a few will be saved, most will be damned!

Today many in the mainline Protestant churches will not be part of this extreme evangelical type of eschatologization of mission. For Reformed churches, it would contradict their focus on history and the earth we live in. If the only mission of the church were to convert as many as possible, the actual situation that people live in is hardly of importance. Here is a negative view of history.

In quite a few circles of Protestantism, there is hardly any feeling for eschatology. The focus is on life here and now. There is variation in consequences. There are those who see the world fully secularized. God actually has not much to do with how things go: politically, economically, socially, and so forth. Faith is something for personal empowerment. The narrative aspect of the Bible is most essential. The psychological dimension of pastoral work comes first. On the other hand, where eschatology is of no importance, the main focus is on the present state of affairs of history. Human history is the platform where action is needed. It is a matter of debate in what sense God is the actor or whether first and foremost we ourselves are the actors. However, the question here is how the mission of the church can ever be understood without an eschatological dimension.

Missio Dei

God makes himself known to the world. This revelation is the first aspect of his mission. God makes his going through history his people's going through history. God makes himself known to the world through women and men, who speak about their experiences of how God acts in their lives. These voices are poetic, prophetic, intellectually convincing, not uttering words but active in caring, politically involved or marginal, and thus being strong although being weak (2 Cor. 12:10). One voice has spoken and made God known as never before and as never thereafter, since there is no need for that. That voice, the voice of Jesus of Nazareth, called his followers to be active throughout the world, making God known to all everywhere. The early church followed in his footsteps and did nothing other than being part of this mission to the world. Since they expected Jesus to come back soon to restore the kingdom of God, they wanted to use the period of waiting as effectively as possible. But not long thereafter it became clear that the period of waiting would be much longer than first expected. Being part of the world was something that had to be developed much more. Conversion could not only be a turning point for the future; it also had to be a life of reconciliation, justification, and sanctification. The process of people to be actors in God's mission had to go on, and a change of lifestyle had to make that visible as the consequence of learning Christ (Eph. 4:20).

The church is an institution that is part of God's mission. It is not the only place of God's mission to the world. It is sometimes not the best place, especially when the church has forgotten that God remains the first actor in his mission. However, if the church is not part of God's mission, it cannot rightly be called a church. The church needs to have an outreach to the world. Especially within the Reformed tradition, this has been highly valued in being very actively part of the actual context in which the church lives. Sometimes this went so far that the distinction between the church and the world was hardly visible anymore. Within the wider context of churches in their global ecumenical gatherings, some have asked the Reformed community to explain in what sense they were preserving their identity as Reformed church. It should be mentioned here also, however, that in some Reformed circles the focus on the world was more expressed in terms of condemning the world.

For the World Alliance of Reformed Churches, it has been an ongoing challenge to be part of God's mission to the world, with a strong focus on the widest context in which the church lives, while at the same time keeping the distance by knowing that the church's reason of existence lies not in the world. It may be helpful to experience this tension in a fruitful way by reflecting on how being conscious of the eschatological dimension of God's mission to the world can go together with a strong focus on the world of which the church is a part.

The Accra Confession and the World in Which We Live

In 2004 at the General Council in Accra, the World Alliance of Reformed Churches adopted the Accra Confession as a document with an outspoken position toward the global economy. It can be regarded as the climax of a long process of covenanting for justice. The strong focus of the document addresses the world we live in; at the same time the language has what could be called "apocalyptic" dimensions. It speaks of the signs of the time. The paragraph under that heading starts thus: "We have heard that the creation continues to groan, in bondage, waiting for its liberation." With an almost unknown fullness of examples of the sad state of affairs, it makes clear that the cry for justice has never been so loudly heard. All voices that could distract from hearing this cry for justice should be silent. Even the voices from heaven come to silence, it seems, in order to hear this loud prayer, with all its contents being laid before God. This prayer leads to an awareness of the mission to which the churches should commit themselves. It is the mission to covenant for justice. It looks clear that here mission goes together with a full eschatological dimension. However, for a continuing process along the lines of the Accra Confession that takes seriously the eschatological dimension, what is needed is a more robust theological foundation.

Justice and Justification

In the New Testament, we read of the parable of the Laborers in the Vineyard. At the end of the day, all workers get the same amount. It does not make any difference whether they have worked a full day or just one hour. They all receive the same amount. Jesus lets us know that this is regarded as unjust, a feeling most readers of this parable have experienced and still experience. Jesus also tells us what the owner of the vineyard replies upon hearing the complaints of those laborers who worked the full day. He says to them: "Am I not allowed to do what I choose with what belongs to me? Or are you envious because I am generous?" (Matt. 20:15).

In this parable there is an absolutely equal distribution of wealth regardless of how much people have worked for it. In any economic system, this would have been regarded as unjust. Not even in the strictest communist society was there an absolutely equal distribution. It can be questioned whether Jesus offers an economic model in this parable. But at least he focuses on what is more than an economic model. This parable tells us about God's gift of grace. This gift of grace is the basis for our justification. We are all justified because we all stand as sinners before God, and to be reconciled with him means that we all need the same amount of justification. We all receive the same daily wage—not because we have worked so hard for it, but because Jesus worked so hard; it even killed him!

The usual daily wage for the work of justification is life, in a true holistic sense and with the quality of eternity. Concerning eternal life, there is an absolutely equal distribution. You cannot have less or more eternal life. Justification is the basis of our life before God. That life is sanctified. And that sanctification can only be made visible in a life of justice. The total of human justice, *justitia humana*, is a holy matter. When a church, or an organization of churches, cries out for justice, that cry for justice can only be made clear with the assumption that this cry for justice is a holy matter. In a document that has as its content a cry for justice, however, one should always start with a biblical and theological foundation to this cry for justice to make clear that this is part of God's work. God has sanctified us to cry out for justice. For an organization of churches, only this biblical and theological foundation can give weight to our cry for justice. It should not start with an economic or political analysis of the situation or—worse—it should not limit itself to such an analysis only. A church statement does not receive its weight from a "secular" analysis. It receives its weight from a thorough biblical and theological foundation.

During the Second World War, the German theologian Dietrich Bonhoeffer (1906–45) became involved in the movement of resistance against Hitler and the Nazi regime. His commitment to resistance against an ungodly regime would not exclude violence, even if that meant killing. He used the example that when a drunk driver on the *Kurfürstendamm* creates victims, one should not first help by giving pastoral care to those lying on the street. What is first and foremost needed is to get the drunk driver out from behind the steering wheel, even if that means an act of violence. It was clear what Bonhoeffer meant. It looks as if he justifies himself in what he said. However, Bonhoeffer made it very clear that we have to act sometimes in the way he said. We have to act, but we stand as sinners before God. Only he can justify us. If one justifies one's own deeds, that justification cannot be final. It is only preliminary. Also this understanding is embedded in the Christian definition of "justification." It begins and ends with God justifying us. So what does this mean when churches are allies in seeking justice? What does this mean when churches condemn acts or structures of injustice? What does this mean when churches develop a theology of justice? What does this mean when churches are socially active, doing work wherein justice is being done? It means that they see this as something preliminary. They do not see it as something absolute. They do not see it as something final. Even in condemning global economic structures, churches should be aware that all are, as Luther said, *simul justus et peccator*, "at the same time righteous and sinful." One church should not condemn the Other without this understanding. A church should not condemn the world without this understanding.

Will this not mean that the voice of the cry for justice will be weakened? Yes, if one thinks that this voice can only have strength when "you see the speck in your neighbor's eye, but do not notice the log in your own eye" (Matt. 7:3). Victims of injustice should cry out against their oppressors, and it is God's call to us to help them to raise their voice or sometimes to raise our voice for them. But no person should deprive oneself of the dignity of being honest about oneself. And also, no one should take away that dignity from the Other. By being honest to God and so being honest to oneself, human justice is something holy because God will give its final justification. It gives the church freedom in the strongest way according to the needs of the times. The church can never give up on God's mission to hear the call to justice because then sanctification will no longer be made visible. Then also justification has become an end process instead of the start of a new life.

The mission of the church, with its focus on the world, has its foundation in God's work of justification and sanctification. Because of this, the church's mission has an eschatological dimension of God's ultimate goal: the coming of his kingdom.

Conclusion

Silence in heaven has the symbolic meaning of the church being active within God's mission. It also means that there is an eschatological thrust to do this work. This should not be seen in the literal way of seeing the end of times being near us in time. The mission of the church has the strongest focus possible on the world we live in. It is, however, done within the context of the grace of God, who will look at what we do from the perspective of the fulfilment of time. Surely for a global organization of churches, there is the ongoing call to be aware of the eschatological dimension of its mission.

PART 2

Covenanting for Justice in the Economy and the Earth

On Justice

Chapter 9

The Accra Confession as a Resource
for Transformation

SETRI NYOMI

Do not be conformed to this world, but be transformed by the renew-
ing of your minds, so that you may discern what is the will of God—
what is good and acceptable and perfect.

(Rom. 12:2)

We live in a world in which conformity to the world and the world's standards is the norm. Christians are afraid to do the will of God. "Sin" has
dropped out of the vocabulary even for Christians because it seems politically incorrect to mention it. If the world's economic systems value greed
and neglect the cries of the poor, many Christians uncritically follow suit. We
live in these kinds of challenging times, when it is so much easier to conform
to the values of the world.

Yet Paul's words still ring true today: "Do not be conformed to this
world, but be transformed." It is a call for all to examine personal and public
lifestyles in the light of the Word of God. Such an examination is done by
Reformed Christians in the light of the Word of God and taking seriously the
signs of the times. The Word of God has further been articulated in Christian
creeds and confessions as good guides to keep belief and lifestyle in tune
with the Word of God. For Reformed Christians, confessions have significance for the following reasons:

1. To counter the false doctrines of the era. In the sixteenth and seventeenth
   centuries, these were often perceived as related to Roman Catholic doctrines and traditions: on papacy, relationships between works and grace,
   understanding of the Bible, the nature of the church, and so forth.

2. To account for the faith, and give a clear articulation of what is believed.
3. In its importance for teaching sound doctrine. This is why some confessions were accompanied by catechisms.

Classical creeds such as the Apostles' Creed and the Nicene Creed give us the basic articulation of beliefs. Historic confessions, such as the Westminster, Heidelberg, Helvetic, and others, came in time to respond to challenges that could have led Christians to conform to contemporary trends uncritically. Modern-day confessions continue to lead in the same direction. In that spirit, the Barmen Declaration, the Belhar Confession, and the Accra Confession continue to be key expressions of how we are linked across time and geography. They represent a commitment to covenanting for life with implications for our lifestyles.

Covenanting for Life

Presbyterian and Reformed churches (churches of the Reformation) in general understand themselves as covenantal communities. We have been received into God's family by grace through faith in Jesus Christ. Christians are placed in a covenantal relationship with God. We are not alone. We belong first to God, but also to the community of believers. The family that belongs to the World Alliance of Reformed Churches alone represents more than 75 million Christians. If we are a covenantal family, then what happens to sisters and brothers in Africa, Latin America, Asia, and any other place ought to affect their sisters and brothers in North America, Europe, and Australia, and vice versa. This ought to have implications for lifestyles. Covenanting for life is therefore an important aspect of Christian living and belonging together.

People of the Reformation tradition usually covenant on the basis of Scripture. One of the Scripture passages that has guided Christians through the ages but has had special emphasis in the life of WARC in the last few years is around John 10:10. There we have our Lord's affirmation that he came so that we may have life in fullness. This is the focus of our covenanting. The theme of life is echoed throughout the Bible, Old and New Testaments. One can recall the clear options given the people of Israel in Deuteronomy 30, between choosing life and good or death and evil. Twentieth-century confessions such as the Barmen Declaration and the Belhar Confession have this commitment at their base.

The Situation in the World Today

As the first decade of the twenty-first century has ended, the world is faced with many challenges. While many are faced with food crises and many cannot even afford one decent meal a week, others have in abundance and are wasting. In the last months of the year 2008, financial markets—major players in the global economic arrangements—began facing a major crisis. While the more affluent countries were slow in locating a couple of billion dollars needed to address the needs of the suffering poor in many countries faced with hunger, those same countries quickly found hundreds of billions of dollars to bail out financial institutions.

The question is clear: "Can people of faith be satisfied with how things operate in the world today?" When one examines the state of the world today by the measuring rod of faith, can one believe that it is good to sit quietly back in satisfaction because everything is consistent with God's will for life? In the 1930s, when churches in Germany saw that a particular ideology endangered the lives of millions of people and that without vigilance the church could be drawn into this evil, the Confessing Church emerged. The Barmen Declaration remains a giant monument, witnessing to the courageous actions of those who know what it means to covenant for life. If God is indeed sovereign over all of life, how can believers stand it when, in this twenty-first century, large groups of people suffer and die because of the way the world's economy is arranged and because of all the distortions? How can believers stay silent when many people living in these situations attend the churches with which we are in communion?

Millions are forced to subsist on less than one dollar a day. A large number of them do not have anything to eat for the most part of each week. There is a lack of access to clean water while privatization of water is going on to enrich a few. Health care is out of reach for many families in the global South. A good education is available only to those who can afford it. In the early part of the first decade of the twenty-first century, a country like Argentina, which was praised for being an "emerging market," suffered a severe economic crash. Countries that have been praised by the World Bank and IMF for macroeconomic successes have often seen an increase in the suffering of their own people. The Structural Adjustment Programs dictated by these institutions have often led to increasing misery in Africa, Asia, and Latin America, including job losses that come as a result of downsizing, and so forth. They have also led to diminished access to education and health for those increasing numbers who cannot afford to pay for such services.

Historically, the Reformed faith has rightly taught that believers cannot stay silent in the face of these realities. The response of covenanting for life against death and destruction is consistent with being Reformed.

When the World Alliance of Reformed Churches gathered at its 24th General Council in Accra, Ghana, in August 2004, it reaped from the years of working in covenantal relationships on justice in the economy and on the earth. With the theme "That All May Have Life in Fullness," this covenant led among, other things, to the Accra Confession.

The Accra Confession is one attempt to expose the false doctrines of our days. Today's false doctrines include limiting God's sovereignty to a narrowly defined spiritual realm. If we had followed these false doctrines in the 1930s in the face of Nazism, or in the decades of apartheid in South Africa, our witness would have been tarnished. Can we apply this standard to issues brought on by the ways in which *oikounomos* takes place in God's world? Let us remember that both *oikoumenē* and *oikounomos* come to us from the same root: *oikos*. Believers cannot yield to the rather mediocre view in which the powers that manage God's household today convince people that individual needs and greed are more important than the needs of the community, and that privatization and the motif of unbridled profit are paramount even if they oppress large numbers of people. Without a critical analysis, we could be engaged in an idolatry in which particular economic systems become gods and pose the only solution. Such idolatry is in part responsible for the global economic meltdown experienced in the dying years of the first decade of the twenty-first century.

Reformed Faith and Economics

The English word "economics" takes its roots from the same Greek word from which ecumenics/ecumenical takes its roots. They both have to do with *oikos*, the household. Economics has to do with managing the household. When we think about the household, we also need to keep in mind *koinōnia*. The household is managed for the sake of the community. Therefore any economic doctrine or practice that breaks the community (especially the covenantal community) stands under judgment. Any economic system that does not foster right relationships is doing something other than managing the household properly.

The Bible (both Old and New Testaments) has much to say about managing the household so that all may live in peace, each under one's own fig tree. The picture given in the Bible shows God as placing special value on taking care of the poor, the marginalized, and the stranger, and the Bible calls for management systems that take everyone into account.

There are many references to ensuring that strangers in the midst of God's people are not neglected. Ancient Hebrew culture has many laws to ensure this. For example, certain laws pertain to harvesting in such a manner that some grains are left. Thus even the poor could go to a field that had just been harvested and be sure to gather something for their meal (cf. the book of Ruth).

In the New Testament are many pointers to the scandal of treating the rich with more respect than the poor. Even the parable of the Last Judgment (the sheep and the goats) lifts up practical commitments and actions to "the least of these" as what the Lord is looking for as a sign of faith (Matt. 25:31–45). In defining his mission, Jesus indicated his coming to release from captivity those who were imprisoned, to free the oppressed, to open the eyes of the blind (Luke 4:18–21). These are all values that contradict popular views of managing the household, views in which the strong, the rich, and the influential are those who receive all the attention.

So the biblical evidence points to God caring for the plight of those who suffer and calls on believers to show this kind of care, thus challenging household systems that do not exhibit this care.

Reformed ancestors such as John Calvin articulate this. Sociologists such as Max Weber have grossly misread Calvin and what they described as the Protestant ethic. The labeling of Calvin as the father of capitalism is a gross misrepresentation of a person whose faith and works point to some other values. Calvin himself was a refugee, an exile from France. There is much evidence that he was close to the refugee community and was a key advocate for their rights. In the late 1950s and early 1960s, André Bieler helped us rediscover Calvin's social thoughts.

Maybe what those sociologists misread was the strong emphasis that Calvin and other Reformers placed on hard work. Hard work is very important in the Reformed family. But Reformed faith has no reason to use this as an excuse to blame the poor for their poverty. On the continent of Africa, for example, there are many hardworking people who are unable to find work or to earn a decent living because of how the global economy is arranged and because economic structural adjustment solutions dictated by institutions such as the IMF and the World Bank continue to render some diligent Africans unemployed. We cannot blame hardworking farmers who are driven out of business because of World Trade Organization (WTO) rules. While their counterparts in many countries of the global North enjoy subsidies that enable them to have an unfair advantage, the African and Asian farmers can hardly get their investments back at the end of each farming season. Meanwhile, the IMF doctrine does not allow governments to offer subsidies. In any case, the governments cannot afford to.

How can Reformed Christians stay silent when the way the household is managed leads to death for some people in the household? This question lies behind the development of the Accra Confession in the 24th General Council of the World Alliance of Reformed Churches.

The Accra Confession

In the tradition of Reformed confessions, the Accra Confession is a response to how we read three things:

1. The Word of God
2. The meaning of our faith
3. The signs of our times, including the cries of the people

These three are very critical ingredients of a true Reformed confession. They were, therefore, important pillars for the Accra Confession. The Accra Confession did not just emerge overnight. It came as a result of a long process of deliberations. For example, having analyzed the world situation, the 22nd General Council, meeting in Seoul in 1989, wrote a letter to young people, indicating how we have failed them by giving them the economy they are being forced to inherit. Then there were regional consultations in 1995 and 1996 that prepared the way for the *processus confessionis* in 1997 at our 23rd General Council in Debrecen, Hungary. What followed were more consultations. The most important ones were held in Buenos Aires (2003) and London Colney (2004). These paved the way for the General Council in Accra, Ghana, which approved the Accra Confession.

Three major principles are noteworthy in the Accra Confession. First, we were careful to recognize that in the Reformed family many would like to ensure that the term "confession" is applied only to what are clearly seen as doctrinal issues. The WARC member churches have different views regarding this interpretation, and therefore we felt a clear need to define how we use the word "confession." It is to express an urgent and active faith response to the major challenge of our times. It is contrary to our faith to remain silent or refuse to act in the face of current economic systems, which are literally killing people, especially in our parts of the world. This is where the confession begins, and the integrity of our faith is at stake.

Second, the Accra Confession has a two-step move in each verse. "We believe, therefore we reject." We are not simply the bandwagon of "anti-s," rejecting everything that does not fit our social outlook. No, it is not merely an NGO declaration. It is a confession made by people of faith as a result of their faith. Therefore the basis of what we say no to should be what we believe, documented biblically. This move is therefore very important. It is what leads us to reject anything that is contrary to the faith we have.

Third, it concludes with a commitment. This is not a convenient set of nice words to recite on Sunday and with which to soothe our consciences. It places demands on us. It is humbling: we too, churches and church structures, individuals and groups in churches, we all need to acknowledge that we stand in judgment under the claims of faith inherent in this confession. Therefore a commitment on our part is called for. Hence the last part. Among other things, the Accra Confession asserts:

> *We believe* in God, Creator and Sustainer of all life, who calls us as partners in the creation and redemption of the world. We live under the promise that Jesus Christ came so that all might have life in fullness (John 10:10). Guided and upheld by the Holy Spirit, we open ourselves to the reality of our world. *We believe* that God is sovereign over all creation. "The earth is the Lord's, and the fullness thereof" (Psalm 24.1 KJV). *Therefore, we reject* the current world economic order imposed by global neoliberal capitalism and any other economic system, including absolute planned economies, which defy God's covenant by excluding the poor, the vulnerable, and the whole of creation from the fullness of life. We reject any claim of economic, political, and military empire that subverts God's sovereignty over life and acts contrary to God's just rule.

Challenges for Presbyterians and Reformed Christians

If the Christian faith calls us all to covenant relationship, then how faith is lived out needs to be seen in action, not simply captured in fine words in a document. Therefore, the significance of the Accra Confession is not so much in the beauty of ideas captured in a document but more in its implications for the lifestyles of people of faith. It calls on believers to yield to God's work of transformation. What affects human beings in Bangladesh, Nairobi, Buenos Aires, Calcutta, Beirut, Accra, Antananarivo, Johannesburg, and other places ought to be of concern to believers everywhere: "When one member suffers, [we] all suffer" (1 Cor. 12:26). But those who suffer are not only in those parts of the world. We have many homeless and jobless people in New York,

Chicago, Amsterdam, Detroit, London, Zurich, Toronto, and other places. What has happened as a result of the economic meltdown ought to be of concern to believers everywhere. Our reflections should not be focused around how to bail out the financial institutions, but on how to mediate life for the millions of ordinary people whose lives have been compromised.

The Accra Confession is a move in which Christians covenant in obedience to God's will, as an act of faithfulness, in mutual solidarity and accountable relationships. This is no easy task. The obvious question is this: Can churches and believers stand up in faith and be courageous enough to adopt the Accra Confession, with all its demands? As we are faced with the global challenges of today, our staying silent or refusing to act is not an option consistent with faith.

The General Council in Accra called upon all WARC member churches, on the basis of our covenanting relationship, to undertake the difficult and prophetic task of interpreting this confession to local congregations and urged all to dare to live by its demands. This is a part of the ecumenical task relevant for the twenty-first century.

Chapter 10

Building a 21st-Century Beloved Community

Using Reformed Bricks and the Mortar of Justice

BERNICE POWELL JACKSON

I count it as an honor to be asked to contribute to this Festschrift in gratitude for the life and ministry of the Rev. Dr. Clifton Kirkpatrick. I have
long admired Cliff's commitment to justice and the church ecumenical, his
wisdom and eloquence. When you add his warmth, his down-to-earth plain-
spokenness, you get that wonderful creation of God named Cliff. Thank you,
Cliff, for all that you have done and all that you will do, not only for the
Reformed church family, but also for all of God's family. May God continue
to bless you and use your many gifts to build the kingdom of God.

It was a moment that few participants would ever forget. But struck especially
hard were the 24th General Council participants from Jamaica and the United
States, especially African Americans. Standing in the "slave castles," really
dungeons, where Africans bound for slavery in the Americas were held on the
west coast of Ghana, we could sense the incredible pain and tangibly feel the
pervasive evil, even centuries later. What was especially painful was the presence of the church in these horror chambers: chapels built above the male dungeons and the courtyards where women slaves were brought to be "selected"
by their captors. The church, the Reformed church, was in the midst of the
Atlantic slave trade, and it was not there to minister to the captives.

The General Council participants were there to come face-to-face with one
shameful part of our Reformed history, to acknowledge how the church sided
with the oppressors instead of the oppressed, and to confess the sins of our
ancestors in the faith. It was a powerful moment in the life of the Reformed
church family, one that in many ways was necessary for us to move forward
in the twenty-first century, not freed from the sin of racism, but having confronted our past in order to more honestly face the future.

More than a decade before the 24th General Council, our Reformed brothers and sisters from South Africa took similar steps as they confronted the church's past defense of the apartheid system and became outspoken critics of apartheid. Through its Kairos document, the churches in South Africa became leaders in the struggle for justice and enabled the country to move forward into a new South Africa.

Indeed, from the earliest days of the Reformed tradition, part of the understanding of faithfulness to the gospel means that we must be immersed in "doing justice, loving kindness, and walking humbly with God" (Mic. 6:8). Moreover, our commitment to the open Communion table means that we are called by our understanding of our faith to be an inclusive community.

One of the most well-known twentieth-century American theologians and preachers was Dr. Martin Luther King Jr., who envisioned the Beloved Community, drawn from the promise of God as written in Isaiah 65:

> For I am about to create new heavens,
>   and a new earth;
> The former things shall not be remembered
>   or come to mind. . . .
> The wolf and the lamb shall feed together,
>   The lion shall eat straw like the ox. . . .
>   They shall not hurt or destroy on all my holy mountain.
> (Isa. 65:17, 25)

Growing out of his years of leadership in the civil rights movement, Dr. King challenged the church as well as society to become the Beloved Community, where all are welcomed to God's table. His was a dream where people of all races come together, where poverty is overcome, where war is no more. He believed that building this Beloved Community was the key to our future: "Western civilization is particularly vulnerable, . . . for our material abundance has brought us neither peace of mind nor serenity of spirit."

As we in the Reformed tradition do our own dreaming for the twenty-first century, perhaps we might start with Dr. King's construct of the Beloved Community and expand its understanding so that all barriers are removed and so that all of God's good creation might be included. Thus, our Reformed understandings of the call of our faith might become the bricks with which we build the Beloved Community, and our response to God's requirement of faith to "do justice" might become the mortar.

Our twenty-first-century Beloved Community must have four cornerstones, I believe. The first is economic justice. We live in a world where the annual income of the richest 1 percent of the world is equal to the annual income of the poorest 57 percent, and where every day twenty-four thousand die from poverty and malnutrition. In his own announcement of his call to ministry, Jesus said, "I come to bring good news to the poor" (cf. Luke 4:18–21), and so must the churches. As people around the world suffer under extreme poverty while others are able to increase wealth, we cannot remain silent. The Accra Confession was adopted at the General Council and commended to our churches for study and action. Yet we know that it was a word not easily received in some parts of the world.

But the near collapse of our global economic system over the past months serves as a wake-up call and an opportunity for the churches in the North to engage in a conversation about an economic system that has created few winners at the expense of many losers. Indeed, the global economic crisis has caused at least an additional twenty-two children to die every hour in 2009, and the church cannot remain silent. We must become an active part of the global conversation in how we put back together our global economic system in a more just way. The president of the World Bank reminds us that "in London, Washington, and Paris, people talk of bonuses or no bonuses. In parts of Africa, South Asia, and Latin America, the struggle is for food or no food." The church cannot remain silent. We can begin to talk about the human vision of scarcity versus God's vision of abundance. We can reject a culture of consumerism and materialism. We can talk about what privatization of public utilities and natural resources really means, especially to the poorest of the poor. We can talk about how we expend our natural resources and what sustainable living is really about. And then after all the conversation, we must begin to build a new global community upon a foundation of economic justice, partnering with civil society to create institutions that serve the poor, overcome poverty, and hold us all accountable to each other.

The second cornerstone of this new Beloved Community is closely tied to the first. We must truly become stewards of God's whole creation and take seriously climate change and global warming. While some in our global family delay addressing global warming, others are already losing their island homes or enduring lasting droughts. As people of faith, we are called to protect our environment, and we must also work for environmental justice and a world where people of color are no longer disproportionately impacted by the dumping of toxic wastes or environmental degradation. As people of faith, we are called to create new models for sustainable living that help to give life to the earth as well as all its people, and to find ways for the church in all its settings to become actively involved in this life-giving task.

Our third cornerstone must be to continue the work already begun to ensure a world of racial justice and equality. Surely the world has made progress in this, and the election of an African American president in the United States is one evidence of this. But we know that in the United States there are still a disproportionate number of people of color incarcerated and that public education is rightly called the twenty-first-century civil rights issue. We know that communities of color in Europe still face housing and job discrimination. We know that indigenous people around the world struggle for their rights. We know that Dalit people in India still fight an unjust and violent caste system. The voice of our Reformed family will be critical to this important antiracist work, and without this work there can be no Beloved Community.

The final cornerstone must be becoming a truly inclusive community. This means taking seriously the call of our brothers and sisters with disabilities to eliminate barriers that keep them from fully participating in the Beloved Community. This means fully including people of all sexual orientations in the church. This means fully including women in all settings of the church. Dr. King said that an injustice anywhere is a threat to justice everywhere. Until we are all at the Welcome Table, none of us can be at the table.

This dream of the Beloved Community can become a reality, and we in the Reformed tradition are called to make it so. We can overcome, and we can begin today.

Chapter 11

The Politics of Power

Negotiating North-South Tensions over Empire and Economics

REBECCA TODD PETERS

Poverty and Inequality in the Twenty-first Century

Poverty is a remarkable constant in the history of human existence. Every age, culture, and human community that has ever existed has had to struggle with the allocation of resources and the unpredictable character of the natural world. Though it is true that egalitarian political structures have shaped some indigenous communities, the vast majority of human history and culture is a reflection of Jesus' words, "You always have the poor with you" (Mark 14:7; Matt. 26:11). However, Jesus' description of the presence of poverty should not be mistaken for his acceptance of economic injustice as a given in our world. To the contrary, Jesus' very life and ministry reflect his mission to disrupt the status quo and show his followers an alternative way of living that offers abundant life for all.

At the dawn of the twenty-first century, we find ourselves in the midst of a world of plenty without the political will to ensure the just distribution of our resources in ways that would witness to the fullness of life that Jesus promised. Bread for the World estimates that 1.02 billion people in the world go hungry, and every five seconds a child dies from hunger-related causes.[1] Global inequality in our world, both between countries and within countries, has increased sharply over the past thirty years, and the rampant consumerism of the first world in the midst of the starvation of countless of our brothers and sisters in the two-thirds world flies in the face of Christian teachings of compassion and justice. In every country across the globe, Reformed Christians recognize the travesty of justice that hunger and poverty represent in our contemporary world.[2] Furthermore, there is widespread agreement

57

within the Reformed family that fighting poverty and economic injustice is a significant mandate of the gospel and an appropriate task for international ecumenical cooperation.

Just as there are principled disagreements in the secular world when it comes to diagnosing the causes of poverty and articulating meaningful strategies to address poverty and human deprivation, within the Reformed family we find ourselves facing quite similar differences of opinion that threaten the very bonds of ecumenical solidarity we have sought to build and repair in the modern ecumenical movement. In this essay, I examine the politics that shape the debate over the Accra Confession within the World Alliance of Reformed Churches (WARC) family and argue that the unique nature of the ecumenical movement offers Christians an essential space for discussing and negotiating serious differences of perspective and opinion regarding the challenges of poverty and wealth in our world today.

The Accra Confession

The Accra Confession represents a remarkably bold and potentially prophetic stand by the Reformed churches on the persistent problems of economic injustice and inequality that plague our world. It pulls no punches in naming the dominant economic and social order as the root of injustice:

> As seekers of truth and justice and looking through the eyes of powerless and suffering people, we see that the current world (dis)order is rooted in an extremely complex and immoral economic system defended by empire. In using the term "empire," we mean the coming together of economic, cultural, political, and military power that constitutes a system of domination led by powerful nations to protect and defend their own interests.[3]

The statement itself presents an unflinching critique of the reigning economic strategies of deregulation, privatization, and trade that have driven the global economy since the early 1980s. Some critics have rejected the Accra Confession for what they charge is its overtly ideological and polemical nature. As this quote demonstrates, the Accra Confession is both ideological and polemical in that it represents a particular vision for a different world order, based on the biblical principle of social justice (its ideological side), and it challenges the apparent dominance of economic neoliberalism as the best pathway out of poverty (its polemical side). Furthermore, it engages in a political critique of first-world countries that have wedded "economic, cultural, political, and military power" into systems of domination, which are named as "empire." Despite the criticism, the text of the Accra Confession accurately represents the majority perspectives that have emerged from twenty years of dialogues, consultations, studies, and encounters that have occurred since Milan Opočenský first put economic justice at the center of the WARC agenda in 1989, when he became general secretary of WARC. However, the statement is not a compromise document, and it does not try to represent the dissenting voices or tensions that have surfaced in the process. The tensions that exist within the ecumenical community over the Accra Confession are largely, though not exclusively, tensions between churches in the global North and churches in the global South.[4]

Points of Tension

Though space does not allow a significant examination of these tensions, I will lay out four major areas of tension that have marked debates about economic justice within WARC over the past twenty years.[5] These tensions reflect disagreements over ideology, theology, process, and power.

Ideological Tensions

Some theologians, economists, and church leaders, primarily from Europe and North America, have issued strong critiques of the content of the Accra Confession, charging that the economic system named as "neoliberalism" in the confession is a caricature that does not correspond to any legitimate and recognizable economic theory. Others have essentially supported the dominant economic perspective by arguing that in an integrated global economy, the only way to help countries in the two-thirds world rise out of poverty is through capitalist economic development that offers the possibility for increased wealth in poor countries. Finally, many WARC members in churches in the global North fundamentally disagree with the definition and rhetoric of "empire" that has dominated ecumenical critiques from the global South for the past several years. These disagreements reflect a dismissal of the value of the concept of empire both on an empirical level as a pragmatic description of the functioning of contemporary global political power as well as a rejection of the use of the term on a metaphorical level to describe the effects of the power of the first world vis-à-vis the developing world.

Theological Tensions

The idea for a *status confessionis* came out of the 1995 consultation in Kitwe, Zambia, where the gathered African leaders interpreted the systematic exclusion of Africa from the world economy and the dominance of the global economic powers in the world as an elevation of structures of society to a level of sovereignty that rightly belongs only to God. The consultation participants at Kitwe declared the system of the global economy idolatrous and called on WARC to denounce these structures of sin. This theological denunciation of the global powers and economic structures was intentionally developed in the spirit of the Barmen and Belhar statements, which both addressed pressing social problems of their day through confessional stances.[6] Serious theological disagreements about the attempts to make the Accra Confession a *status confessionis* came largely from churches in Western Europe. There were three primary critiques of the *status confessionis* model. First, some people fundamentally disagreed with the perspective of the churches in the South that an economic system can be "immoral," and consequently they rejected the notion that our current economic system is sinful. Second, others argued that the case of the global economic order is not parallel to either Nazi Germany or apartheid South Africa because there is no formal collusion between state or national churches and a particular political power. Third, some people argued that declaring a *status confessionis* requires the capacity to gather a representative ecumenical council of all branches of Christianity (Protestant, Catholic, and Orthodox) to endorse the *status confessionis*, a feat which is impossible, given the current state of the ecumenical movement.

Tensions over Process

In addition to the ideological and theological tensions over issues of economic and political injustice, some WARC members from the developed world who participated in consultations and meetings as part of the process leading up to and including the 24th General Council meeting have repeatedly expressed their frustration at what they perceived to be a study process marked by a predetermined ideological agenda. Some representatives from European churches expressed their distress at not having their perspectives and concerns seriously engaged during the process leading up to Accra; others felt that they were intentionally shut out of the conversation because their attitudes did not support the critique that was being developed. Other representatives from North America and Europe described their distress over feeling manipulated by the worship themes and liturgy of the 24th General Council meeting as well as by the controlled nature of the meeting, which allowed little room for dialogue over serious points of disagreement.

Tensions over Power

Finally, perhaps the most tense and awkward aspect of this division between churches in the global North and the global South has to do with the shifting nature of power and authority within the ecumenical movement represented by the adoption of the Accra Confession. From the dialogues on "Reformed Faith and Economics" in the 1990s, onward through the debates about whether or not to declare a *status confessionis* that marked the years from the 23rd WARC General Council meeting in Debrecen, Hungary, in 1997 until the 24th General Council meeting in Accra in 2004—the voices, perspectives, and critiques of theologians and church leaders from the global South have been given prominence and authority in ways that have challenged the traditional power politics of the ecumenical movement. For perhaps the first time, a major international ecumenical initiative has been developed and promoted by theologians and church leaders from the global South, over and against the expressed wishes, desires, and judgments of theologians and church leaders from the traditional sources of power in the global North. This accomplishment is all the more significant given the fact that church leaders from the global North have become used to setting the theological and ecumenical agenda. Though the majority of funds supporting WARC continue to come from churches in the developed world, the demographics of church membership are shifting dramatically toward the developing world. At the 24th General Council meeting in Accra, 270 delegates represented 161 churches in the global South, and only 95 delegates represented 30 churches in the global North. It is only reasonable to assume that theological issues and perspectives reflecting the lived reality of Christianity in the global South will and should continue to shape the ecumenical agenda of WARC. This shift, however, promises to be one of the most difficult challenges for the ecumenical movement in the twenty-first century.

Ecumenical Space as Opportunity for Transformation

As a Christian ethicist, I share many of the assumptions, analyses, and critiques that shape the sentiments of the Accra Confession and the subsequent

Covenanting for Justice movement that has been building in recent years. My work is focused on trying to help first-world Christians figure out how to engage and dismantle our privilege and our complicity in injustice in ways that reflect genuine solidarity with poor and marginalized people while also working toward the social transformation of the dominant structures of oppression in our world. I engage in this work within the boundaries of Christian community because, I believe, religious communities offer an opportunity for people to engage in meaningful dialogue and action that offers the possibility for transforming injustice and inequality in our world. Addressing issues of wealth and power are difficult, at best, in the secular world, where differences of opinion can solidify into ideological divisions that preclude genuine engagement and active attention to social transformation and justice. As we have seen in this chapter, ideological tensions and divisions also exist within the church and within the ecumenical movement.

Ecumenical space, however, holds out the possibility of creating a sacred space in which diverse communities can come together around a common commitment to justice, to try to seek transformation and reconciliation. Though the example we have just examined of the Accra Confession demonstrates that ecumenical space does not always honor the sacred, respect diversity, or agree on what constitutes justice, nevertheless, if the ecumenical movement hopes to further dialogue and develop common ground around the divisive issues of empire and economic injustice that plague our world, we must learn how to respect and embrace the potentiality of our ecumenical space and the opportunities that it affords us to participate in doing God's work.

Ecumenical Space Can Be Sacred

The ecumenical movement offers Christians the opportunity to come together in affirming the foundational teachings of Jesus Christ that call us to service, compassion, and care for our neighbor. When we gather together, bound by our common commitment to Christ, we have the possibility of entering a liminal space, a space outside the traditional divisions of politics and ideology that mark the secular arena. In this way ecumenical space offers the possibility of creating a sacred space that can challenge the human powers of empire and wealth now dominating the political sphere. However, we must remember that God's presence is not automatic or guaranteed simply because we gather in God's name. Honoring sacred space requires that we act toward one another with openness, love, honesty, and a willingness to be transformed by the presence of the sacred in our midst.

Ecumenical Space Should Respect Diversity

As we think about the nature of ecumenical space and the opportunities for ecumenism in the twenty-first century, we remember that diversity is part of God's good creation, and it is a meaningful and valuable aspect of the ecumenical movement. Our diversity of perspectives, cultures, ideas, and experiences offers us the unique opportunity to learn from one another, and our respect for one another as brothers and sisters in Christ ought to shape our interactions in ways that allow for meaningful dialogue across the lines of difference that may separate people in secular settings. The ecumenical movement offers the opportunity to bring people of faith together across the lines of difference that mark contemporary situations of injustice, with the goal of seeking understanding and partnership.

Ecumenical Space Ought to Be Oriented toward Justice

As a space where Christians can come together to engage one another and participate together in living out our calling as followers of Christ, the ecumenical movement should reflect Jesus' ministry and his attention to and concern for the people who live on the margins of society. He healed them, talked with them, and broke bread with them; he taught his followers to care for the hungry, the poor, the naked, and the outcast. Just as Jesus' life and work are shaped by his passion for justice in the world, the ecumenical movement must likewise be shaped and formed toward seeking a justice-oriented world.

The Possibilities of Ecumenical Space

Creating the kinds of ecumenical spaces that can facilitate transformation requires great attention to issues of power, personality, and politics. Ecumenical spaces of dialogue and transformation that are sacred, diverse, and oriented toward justice offer the possibility of promoting meaningful dialogue, especially between Christians in the global North and the global South, over the issues of empire and economic justice that continue to divide us. If theologians and church leaders from the North and the South truly desire to work together to address the problems of political and economic injustice in our world, then it is imperative that we figure out how to create the kind of ecumenical spaces I have described: sacred spaces where we are able to experience the Holy Spirit working among us; diverse spaces where we listen to and honor our differences; and justice-oriented spaces where we join forces to seek the kind of social changes that promote an abundant life for all.

Chapter 12

The King Is Naked

A Voice of Passion in the Cause of Justice

ROBERTO JORDAN

*W*hen thinking of Cliff, what always comes to mind is the frequency with which he refers to "my passions": be it his family, be it ecumenism, be it the church and church unity, or be it the cause of justice. In this sense Cliff has a passionate voice in the cause for justice, with justice, and from justice. This has been particularly relevant in his support and defense of the whole process that led up to the Accra Confession and its prophetic place in the life of the church, generally, and the Reformed churches, particularly.

In this essay, I wish to discuss the difference between a "voice *for*" and a "voice *with*." In doing so, I observe that Cliff has been and continues to be a strong voice with so many who yearn for a new and different reality in the world today.

The term "the voice of the voiceless" is common; a quick Internet search reveals over one million entries! Probably many people have used this concept even with the best of intentions. However, two problems arise: theological and sociological:

1. Theologically: I believe God did not create those with a voice and those with no voice. God's creation was declared "good" by God, and life in fullness is the will of God for all creation—which includes the fact that all have "voice." In this sense I cannot accept as God's will that there should be the "voiceless" in the world.

2. Sociologically: Where some are called "voiceless" it usually refers to the power factor: voices have been silenced, not that they do not have a voice. This power factor has reduced women, children, aboriginal people; people from different cultural, religious, and social backgrounds and options; and so many other people—reduced them to a situation of being oppressed, where the voices that do exist and so express this oppression are often repressed and ignored.

What is fundamental, at least to my understanding, is that no one is voiceless, though it is true that often they have been reduced to a situation such that their voices are not heard or taken into consideration. Yet those voices are there in song, myth, storytelling, dreams, memories, dance, hopes.

This is why I have a serious problem with those who define their role as that of "the voice of the voiceless." To accept this would imply accepting that there are voiceless who need people to speak for them. In reality, what is needed are people who firmly believe that no one is voiceless, and what is really needed is the solidarity to be *a voice with* those who have been silenced and therefore have many things worth saying.

The difference, then, between those who believe they can speak *for* others and those who speak *with* others—the difference is that those who speak for others are accomplices of an imperial system that reproduces oppression, keeping people silent and speaking for them. On the other hand, those who choose to be in solidarity question the oppressive situation; with those who are silenced, they commit themselves to transform the situation in a way so that the silenced voice is no longer silent and can speak its own words, not merely through the words of others.

This issue is illustrated in Hans Christian Andersen's tale *The Emperor's New Clothes* (1837), about an extremely prosperous king who cares more about clothes than people or anything else in the world. Two unscrupulous tailors promise the finest suit of the most beautiful cloth, which they tell the king is invisible to all who are not up to the king's standards. Yet not one person sees the cloth; but nobody wants to be taken for a fool, so all play the game. Finally the king processes the streets of the kingdom, and all admire the emperor's new clothes (though in actual fact he is naked). Suddenly and in true biblical fashion, a child shouts out: "The king is naked!" This opens the eyes of all, even though the king insists on his stupidity and continues in procession, naked though convinced that only he can see the clothes, believing everybody else is stupid.

This story serves as a parable for the cause of justice and the need for clearer voices that will commit to the transformation of unjust situations. It is not surprising that the only one who dares to speak the truth is a child, a child who shouts out the evident truth that all can see but no one speaks: "The king is naked." This breaks the structure of illusion for all but the king himself, who cannot resist the new situation and must continue with the illusion, because what would become of the king if he saw himself vulnerable, naked, fooled by others, the laughingstock of the town?

The current social-economic world situation is similar to that of the king in this tale: he is more interested in his own particular situation and not in the life of the people; he is a prey of unscrupulous tailors, who have sold the trick of the new suit of invisible cloth, one that only fools cannot see. This situation was clearly denounced through the whole process in which the World Alliance of Reformed Churches has been involved for so many years, and particularly in the one that involved the *processus confessionis*, which evolved into the Accra Confession.

The Accra Confession is like this tale of the child who shouts out "The king is naked"; it denounces the crude reality that has only deepened since the 24th General Council (2004) in Accra and has led us to the current economic and social disaster affecting the lives of millions: those who already were suffering and those who have now become sufferers. While much of the structure is only interested in salvaging itself, ignoring the needs of others, billions of dollars are given to firms who prize themselves as courageous and successful in the midst of such a situation. While millions of people continue to suffer, many refuse to fall into despair.

What can be clearly established is that the Accra Confession is not a voice for the voiceless; instead, it is the expression of those who have been forced into silence over so many years, but have refused to be silenced. What we know as the Accra Confession today is the result of the voices of women and men, youth, elderly, young from Africa, Asia, Latin America, together with the voices of those which the empire[1] wanted to silence within its own frontiers. No, the commitment to justice that developed the Accra Confession is not the expression of those who say they speak for the voiceless. On the contrary, it is the voice of these same people of yesterday and of today who cling to the will of God the Creator, have refused to believe they have no voice, and so they have continued to dream, to dance, to share stories, and so to keep faith alive by sharing from generation to generation, knowing, believing it was not in vain, that the silenced voices had not disappeared but were very much alive.

It is not surprising that even today these voices that found expression in the call for justice and the denunciation of injustice are being pushed and battered by forces trying to silence them. Those who—just like the king in the tale, when confronted with the sad reality that the "king is naked"—do nothing to change the situation and turn to the new reality have thus kept on in the procession, hoping that truth would not survive and their nakedness would not be exposed.

What the king does then, while continuing as if no one has denounced the truth ("It was only a kid who shouted out, and who cares what a kid has to say?"), is to try and involve the rest of the people in sterile discussions:

- Who defines reality: the king or the hungry?
- Whose voice will be heard? Those who have "the power"? Those who have been reduced to silence and so are treated as if they do not exist?
- Or let us be progressive and create a "committed" group from around the world that will claim to speak for the voiceless but do little to change the status quo, and while doing this the group contributes to keep the empire alive and kicking. This is a way of saying that "empire" is an ideological figment of some erratic imagination; if we ignore it long enough, it will disappear.

The tale of the king's new clothes is one way to remind us that the voiceless are very much present in history. We can choose to listen to them, or we can choose to ignore them. When accepting the call issued by God to be agents of transformation in the midst of injustice, we recognize the need to keep alive the prophetic voice of women and men, who in the middle of the crisis continue to speak, to dream, to pray, to call out to God that the promise of life in fullness for all is for now, not just for tomorrow.

Against what the "naked kings" of the world today would hope for, the truth is that there are many who will not let voices be silenced and will continue to shout out: "The king is naked." There are many who with passion are committed to transforming the evil, demonic structures of this world into the life-providing structures God has proclaimed as the truth for creation, as it was in the beginning, should be now, and will be for evermore.

Let us pray to God for more and more women and men to increase the "great cloud of witnesses[;] let us also lay aside every weight and the sin that clings so closely, and let us run with perseverance the race that is set before us, looking to Jesus the pioneer and perfecter of our faith" (Heb. 12:1–2). Wherever it is needed and whenever it is needed, with courage and determination, together with those whom the powers have tried to reduce to silence but are still very much a voice in this world—let us shout out with a voice of passion for the cause for justice: "The king is naked!"

I am convinced that Cliff has been and will continue to be a voice of passion in the cause of justice.

Chapter 13

Living Faithfully in the Context of Empire

Challenges and Opportunities

OMEGA BULA

*T*his is a story of how a member church of the World Alliance of Reformed Churches is living out its faith in a context of empire. Throughout its history, the United Church of Canada has lived out its prophetic tradition on cutting-edge issues as part of its Christian faith. Recent positions and statements that reflect this tradition include "Mending the World: An Ecumenical Vision for Healing and Reconciliation" (1997), "To Seek Justice and Resist Evil: Towards a Global Economy for All God's People" (2000), "A Song of Faith: A Statement of Faith of the United Church of Canada" (2006), "Living Faithfully in the Midst of Empire" (2006). At the core of these positions and statements is a careful reflection, analysis, and listening to the increasing pain and misery for the majority of the people in the world and God's Earth community.

The presenting question has been "How will a faithful people become partners in God's mission in this context?" This question calls all faithful people to "a renewed vocation for engagement in God's mission, justice seeking, and transformative ministry in the midst of empire."[1] Our journey as a church has revealed these opportunities to include an understanding of the gospel as an alternative to empire, God's call to engage with the world, and the call to "Covenant for Life in Creation as a new way of naming and re-energising our contemporary continuing commitment to God's reign within the current context of empire."[2] By covenanting, communities of faith in the United Church of Canada are being invited to stand together with those who suffer from systemic injustice and to build new life-giving relationships which engage in the struggle for alternatives to empire.

Background

In August 2000, the 37th General Council of the United Church of Canada approved the report "To Seek Justice and Resist Evil: Towards a Global Economy for all God's People." This report described and analyzed "the global reality of systemic economic injustice" (neoliberal economic globalization) and called the church "to seek justice and resist evil so that together in mission we can build a global economy for all God's people." In their stories on life-giving economies and theological reflection on the current global economic systems, United Church partners in Africa, Asia, the Caribbean, Canada, Latin America, the Middle East, and the South Pacific confirmed the impact and the human face of suffering and increasing environmental degradation. The reflection was critical of the global economic status quo and its exclusionary tendencies; it named the fact that we, their Canadian partners, were complicit in the persistent relationships of domination and suppression through our participation in processes and practices of neoliberal economic globalization and the unlimited market capitalism that sustains our consumer cultures and the building of economic, political, and social-cultural empires.

In November 2004, the General Council Executive of the United Church of Canada meeting affirmed the Accra Confession: Covenanting for Justice in the Economy and the Earth.[3] It urged its Permanent Committee on Programs for Ministry and Mission "to develop a process to engage the United Church courts (conferences, presbyteries, and congregations) in study and action."[4] It was received as a timely prophetic voice, a strengthening of what had been a core message in the report "To Seek Justice and Resist Evil: Towards a Global Economy for All God's People." Through the Justice, Global, and Ecumenical Relations Unit, an Empire Task Group was formed to expand the work of the church on economic globalization. The task group embraced the definition and understanding of empire contained in the Accra Confession. The Accra Confession recognized that neoliberal economic globalization was no longer an adequate concept to describe the current economic crisis and the imperialist power of the dominant politico-economic interests behind this crisis. The World Alliance of Reformed Churches said, "As we look at the negative consequences of globalization for the most vulnerable and for the Earth community as a whole, we have begun to rediscover the evangelical significance of the Biblical teaching about Empire."[5]

Similar analysis was present in the Alternative Globalization Addressing Peoples and Earth (AGAPE) process led by the World Council of Churches. There the question was asked, "How do we live our faith in the context of globalization" and in a time of "empire"? Both the Accra Confession and the AGAPE process called the worldwide church to commit itself "to reflect on the question of power and empire from a biblical and theological perspective, and take a firm faith stance against hegemonic powers because all power is accountable to God."[6]

In 2006, a major report, "Living Faithfully in the Midst of Empire," was approved by the 39th General Council. The Empire Report, as it has come to be known in the United Church and beyond, worked with the understanding of "empire" as global domination, directed by the powerful nations, global economic institutions, and transnational companies. The report challenges systems and structures that perpetuate economic injustice and ecological destruction. It affirms justice for life as a matter of faith and a confessional issue of our time. The General Council called for a continuing education and faith formation within the church in order to build capacity to resist empire and to seek and live out alternatives to empire. A need for transformative justice in church and society was affirmed. At this time a call was made to develop a covenant that witnesses to empire, confesses our complicity, and calls individuals, congregations, and other mission units to commit to living faithfully in the midst of empire.

Engaging Faith Communities in Education for Justice

In the last three years, fulfilling the report "Living Faithfully in the Midst of Empire" has included intensive work focused on education for justice and production of educational resources on empire for use across the church. Central to these processes has been the engagement with the key concerns of theology and faith in the context of empire, pointing to the fact that the threat to life represented by contemporary empire means we are at a critical time, a *kairos*[7] time, for the discernment of the gospel. In addition, much work has been done on (1) deepening the understanding of the complexity of empire as a system of global domination and how we participate, knowingly and unknowingly; (2) coming to terms with our complicity in "empire," primarily through our role as consumers in the global capitalist market system; (3) sharing stories of threats to life and creation from United Church global and Canadian partners, stories that help put a human face on the experiences and impacts of empire; (4) advocacy for economic and ecological justice and support for sustainable communities; (5) accompaniment of partners struggling with the impacts of the economic crisis; and (6) the articulation of a renewed vocation of resistance and transformation.

The use of the term "empire" to help us understand the power of domination in today's world has not been easily accepted by all in our faith communities. We have learned that we can spend much time and get caught up in describing and understanding empire while threats to life and the earth are more and more entrenched. Although conversations and understanding empire remain important for our work together, priority must be placed on creating resistance and alternatives. The current global economic crisis of the capitalist system has helped to bring home to many among us the many faces of empire. According to recent estimates, 53 million people live on less than $2 a day as a result of the global economic crisis. This is in addition to 130–155 million people already pushed into poverty in 2008 because of the food and fuel crisis, with 70 percent of these being women.[8] (1) Ending poverty and inequality; (2) ensuring decent jobs and public services for all; (3) calling us to use stimulus packages to build a green economy and tackle climate change; and (4) addressing inadequate public control and regulation of finance, with a focus on democratizing governance of the global economy—these all are calls to make sense of matters concerning faith in the midst of empire.

Challenges, Opportunities, and Lessons Learned in Our Faith Community

Silence is not an option, whether out of ignorance, paralysis, or the sheer complexity of the issues. Being church calls us to be living participants in God's mission for peace and justice in the world. Living faithfully in the midst of empire means that we must work harder than ever to hear the prophetic call to justice and from our place of privilege and power, to discern what God is calling us to do. Failing to read the signs of the times is tantamount to collaboration with the dominant forces in the world. These are the forces of empire: forces of economic injustice, ecological degradation, and violation of human dignity. These forces have increased poverty for the two-thirds world, the growing gap between the rich and the poor, and are responsible for conflict and war in much of the global South. As a church with abundant resources of people and money, privilege and power, we have a responsibility and are accountable to ensure that the call to the church for public prophetic witness and the struggle for systemic change is lived out in a world groaning in pain from poverty, excessive wealth, environmental degradation, conflict, and social exclusion.

As communities of faith participating in the United Church of Canada, we are learning that *confession*—acknowledging and analyzing the church's complicity in empire—is both a challenge and an opportunity. We have been able to look at our complicity through our participation as individuals, institutions, and nations in empire's systems of domination and control. It is a challenge to apply an empire lens on our self-understanding as a community of faith. A "Song of Faith" adopted at the 39th General Council in 2006 celebrates a church "seeking to continue the story of Jesus by embodying Christ's presence in the world." We sing of a church with a purpose, where "faith is nurtured, hearts comforted, gifts shared for the good of all, resistant to the forces that exploit and marginalise, fierce love in the face of violence, human dignity defended, members of a community held and inspired by God, corrected and comforted, instruments of the loving Spirit of Christ, creation's mending."[9]

How can we live into this song when we struggle with a history of colonization and superior attitudes toward the First Nations people of this land called Canada? Are we able to speak truth to power on the daunting questions of peace in the Middle East? What does it mean to strive for right relations at the heart of God's mission? How can our practice of partnership reflect justice, love, respect, mutuality, reciprocity, and transparency in a context that thrives on domination by those who have power privilege? We are encouraged to take up the challenge of our collective confession by seeking to be a responsive and transformed people of faith, living out hope and love at every level of our being church. With the help of an "empire lens," a tool developed for use in the educational work on empire, communities of faith in our denomination have been called to act with renewed energy on all resolutions made over the past many years, those that challenge imperialism and systemic injustice. These and many more are questions we continue to struggle with as we live faithfully in the context of empire.

This struggle is an opportunity in the sense that confession of our complicity in the systems of injustice leads to deeper analysis and new learning that empowers us for engaging justice work from a "not-feeling-guilty" stance. We are compelled to be humble and self-critical. With humility and self-critical reflection, we are able to move beyond paralysis into the search for renewed patterns and models of engagement in the struggle for life in its fullness. One example has been our ability as a denomination to reconceptualize our work and understanding of ecological justice in a new way, and especially in making linkages with poverty and wealth.

As a member church of the World Alliance of Reformed Churches, we have benefited immensely from the connections with the regional and global ecumenical processes on living out the Accra Confession. We have found space to share our work and struggles in our commitment to live faithfully in the midst of empire. We have also committed to sharing significant financial resources needed to sustain the work on Covenanting for Justice in the economy and the earth within WARC and its ecumenical partners. We have learned that building solidarity and resistance with global partners is critical. As a church with privilege and power, we have much to learn from those who struggle for life. Though global partner stories are heavy with suffering, oppression, and exploitation, they are also filled with a profound sense of hope and resilience. We are only able to name our complicity and to begin to turn around (to repent) through honest and faithful confession of our complicity in the suffering of the body of Christ.

A Covenant for Life in Creation

We live in hope that the journey we have embarked on will take us to transformed spaces as a people of faith living faithfully in the context of empire. We have learned that we cannot remain silent: words alone are not enough. We need actions for justice in the world. We are called to covenant together for a long-term commitment to transformation and the building of sustainable communities. What follows below is a covenant that has gone to the fortieth United Church of Canada General Council in August 2009. It asks the General Council to declare that the United Church of Canada is committed to covenanting to live faithfully in the midst of empire in response to God's covenant with us. Also, it asks the General Council to receive the document Covenanting to Live Faithfully in the Midst of Empire and authorize its use to develop resources for study within the United Church of Canada, including an education process for engaging with the proposed Covenant for Life in Creation.[10]

This is our journey as a denomination, and we are pleased to share it as we move into new space as a Reformed communion of people of faith, committed to justice and peace in our time. We are aware that we are not alone: we live in God's world.

Appendix

4.2 A Covenant for Life in Creation

God's covenant of grace continues to provide abundant life in all of
        creation, and the weaving of right relations sustains life
    and the wholeness of one earth community in all its diversity.
God's gift of life has been distorted and denied through time
    by unrelenting human greed and will for domination
    made manifest in the wasting of the planet's resources,
    that brings suffering, despair, and violence,
    that plagues all peoples, communities, and creatures
        throughout God's world.
We name this complex human-made web of domination: empire
    and hold that the many forms of empire are the primary obstacles
    to God's purposes of justice, equality, and reconciliation
    between peoples, nations, and within creation.
We, the people of The United Church of Canada,
    in response to God's covenant with us,
    covenant to engage in the world,
    to listen to, learn from, and act
    with those of us who suffer,
    who hunger for bread, justice, and compassion;
    and with all of creation,
    to live faithfully in the midst of empire.
We choose to confess our turning away from God
    in the selfish destruction of life and relationships in creation.
This brokenness results in false desires and wrong choices,
    made systemic in an all-consuming global economy
    that victimizes the planet, us,
    the poor, our neighbours, and
    our sisters and brothers worldwide.
Empire leads to poverty and the threat of death for many
    while only a few grow in their wealth and power.
We commit ourselves to turn away from maintaining relationships
    of inequality and oppression.
We especially think of our relationships with Aboriginal peoples
        in Canada. . . .[11]
We trust in God's grace and power to transform us.
We hope and act in and with the Spirit of transformation,
    that the reign of God that Jesus proclaimed and lived,
    crossing barriers of race, class, and gender,
    and finally offered his life for,
    may empower us to new life in love.

We seek the restoration of relationships
    of respect, non-violence, and peace among all people
    and within God's beloved one Earth community in all its diversity.
We embrace God's reign of liberation and compassion
    and will work and witness in the way of solidarity and suffering love,
    the way of the cross and the promise of resurrection,
through how we worship God and seek divine presence in our lives,
    how we make decisions as community,
    how we use the gifts and resources we have been given,
    how we share our faith among ourselves with adults,
        children and youth,
    how we live out God's good news in the world,
    how we seek justice and act for change,
    how we minister to one another and the community and world
        in which we live.
In all these areas we seek
    to choose life, and resist empire,
    to create sustainable alternatives for the common good,
    to form holistic relationships and communities of joy and justice,
    to enact daring discipleship and mutuality on the sacred earth.
We trust in God, Christ and the Spirit,
    grateful for all the prophets and witnesses in faith.
We will care for the future to the seventh generation,
    as we journey from death to new life, from empire
        to one Earth community.
We will learn how to follow Jesus with those who suffer under empire.
Our Creator, the multitude of faithful witnesses, and the
        impoverished and exploited,
    are beloved and trusted companions on the way.
As people of God,
    as part of the worldwide community and God's sacred creation,
we humbly and joyfully covenant to learn to live faithfully
        in the midst of empire
    and respond to God's call for renewed life for all.
God be our guide and helper!

PART 3 *Oikumenē* and *Koinōnia*

On Ecumenism

Chapter 14

A Gift from Islam

"A Common Word between Us and You" and the Lessons from Interfaith Dialogue Today

IAIN TORRANCE

A Common Word between Us and You"[1] (hereinafter, ACW) is an open letter that was sent to Pope Benedict XVI, all Orthodox patriarchs, the Archbishop of Canterbury, and the representative leaders of all the major Christian traditions, including the World Alliance of Reformed Churches, on October 13, 2007. It was authored by 138 Muslim scholars, clerics, and intellectuals who unanimously came together for the first time since the days of the Prophet (PBUH)[2] to declare the common ground between Christianity and Islam. It is easy to overlook the aspect of unanimity here. I believe ACW is as much a document directed internally, to seek unity within Islam, as it is an outward document, seeking dialogue with Christians. The letter is not polemical in tone. Its signatories have adopted the traditional Islamic position of respecting the Christian Scripture and calling Christians to be more, not less, faithful to it. Thus ACW invites Christians to dialogue on the basis that we share belief in one God and have a common commitment to love our neighbor.

I believe this is a historic step and a document of truly immense importance. I believe ACW is to be received as a gift, coming from an ancient religious tradition in which gift-giving is understood as a way of transforming a relationship. Gift-giving is to be distinguished from the so-Western notions of "risk" or "investment." So ACW is a new initiative, given in generosity and love. It is not "a risk."

Why do I understand it in this way? Because the document is neither aggressive nor defensive, but hospitable and friendly, it invites the same kind of response. It testifies to a deep devotion to God, inviting us to search ourselves

Edited and reprinted with permission of the editor of *The Presbyterian Outlook*.

and respond out of the same devotion. ACW pays close attention to the Bible and invites us to respond scripturally and faithfully.

There has been a process of response. A number of us welcomed the letter immediately, sensing its importance. David Ford, Regius Professor of Divinity at Cambridge and one of the leaders of Scriptural Reasoning, the practice whereby Jews, Muslims, and Christians read their Scriptures together, initiated one line of response. This was collegial and profound. We had one session working at the response at Princeton Seminary, inviting several professors to join the discussion. David Ford's draft was brought to a specially called consultation at Lambeth Palace at the beginning of June. The Archbishop of Canterbury subsequently (July 15, 2008) issued his own distinctive and fully reworked response: "A Common Word for the Common Good."[3]

What is at the heart of these responses? *First*, there is close reading and appreciation of what is being said to us. ACW quotes the Shema in the book of Deuteronomy (6:4–5), "Hear, O Israel: The LORD our God, the LORD is one! / You shall love the LORD your God with all your heart and with all your soul and with all your strength*" (TNIV alt.). It also quotes Jesus' affirmation of this, and his uniting of it to the command to love our neighbor:

> Then one of the scribes came, and having heard them reasoning together, perceiving that he had answered them well, asked him, "Which is the first commandment of all?"
>
> Jesus answered him, "The first of all the commandments is: 'Hear, O Israel, the Lord our God, the Lord is one.
>
> 'And you shall love the Lord your God with all your heart, with all your soul, with all your mind, and with all your strength.' This is the first commandment.
>
> "And the second, like it, is this: 'You shall love your neighbor as yourself.' There is no other commandment greater than these." (Mark 12:28–31 NKJV)

This is followed, as David Ford has observed, by a truly remarkable passage, which I quote in full:

> In the light of what we have seen to be necessarily implied and evoked by the Prophet Muhammad's (PBUH) blessed saying: *"The best that I have said—myself, and the prophets that came before me—is: 'There is no god but God, He Alone, He hath no associate, His is the sovereignty and His is the praise and He hath power over all things,'"* we can now **perhaps** understand the words *"The best that I have said—myself, and the prophets that came before me"* as equating the blessed formula *"There is no god but God, He Alone, He hath no associate, His is the sovereignty and His is the praise and He hath power over all things"* precisely with the "First

and Greatest Commandment" to love God, with all one's heart and soul, as found in various places in the Bible. That is to say, in other words, that the Prophet Muhammad (PBUH) was **perhaps**, through inspiration, restating and alluding to the Bible's First Commandment. God knows best, but certainly we have seen their effective similarity in meaning.

I have added emphases and underlining to make the argument stand out. What I hope readers will notice is that the double use of the word "perhaps" here allows for openness, exploration, and dialogue. The acknowledgment that "God knows best" reminds us that our knowledge is always limited. However we are to read this, I believe it represents a remarkable step in interfaith generosity.

Second, in response documents, Christians have rightly and appropriately expounded our own understanding of the love of God. Generally speaking, when ACW speaks of "the love of God," it means "our love *for* God." In the First Letter of John, Christians are given to understand "This is what love is; not that we have loved God, but that God has loved us" (1 John 4:10 alt.) and "We love because God loved us first" (1 John 4:19 alt.). Christians have expounded our understanding of God as Trinity. This does not, we maintain, compromise the unity of God, but by understanding God as a unity of active love, we see ourselves as intensifying and enriching the unity of God. In our response, we Christians have also brought our texts to the table, especially drawing attention to the parable of the Good Samaritan, in which the lawyer's question ("Who is my neighbor?") is turned around in a way that should be definitive for our understanding of neighbor love, and for Jesus' teaching about love of enemies in the Sermon on the Mount.

In October 2008, David Ford and Tim Winter (Abdal Hakim Murad) hosted authors of ACW and Christian respondents at Cambridge University to read Scripture together. The object was to deepen trust and to bring together religious leaders and academic institutions. Rowan Williams subsequently invited the group to Lambeth Palace on October 15, 2008. In a context of mutual welcome and seriousness, we commended a communiqué.[4] Together, we declared:

> As we were meeting together, we were deeply troubled to learn of the situation in Mosul (Iraq) where threats to the Christian community have further added to the tragic Iraqi refugee situation. These threats undermine the centuries-old tradition of local Muslims protecting and nourishing the Christian community, and must stop. We are profoundly conscious of the terrible suffering endured by Iraqi people of every creed in recent years and wish to express our solidarity with them. We find no justification in

Islam or Christianity for those promoting the insecurity or perpetrating the violence evident in parts of Iraq. We call upon the religious, political, and community leaders to do all in their power to promote the return of all persons and communities, including the ancient Christian communities, and ensure a stable environment in which all citizens can flourish. We unequivocally declare that, in Iraq as anywhere else in the world, no person or community should be persecuted or threatened on account of their religious faith. We must all have a particular concern for religious minorities in our midst.

I commend these sentiments and this dialogue to Reformed Christians everywhere. I relate this perspective of costly reconciliation coming as a gift from Islam to the Ecumenical Stance Statement of the PC(USA) that was adopted in 2008 (and note that the editor of this volume was a member of the final drafting team). This statement, one of the last significant documents that resulted from Clifton Kirkpatrick's tenure as stated clerk of the PC(USA), sets out a vision and objectives for ecumenical and interfaith relations for the PC(USA) during the next ten years. It lifts up boldly what previous Stance Statements did not emphasize: a desire to see the expansion of *oikumenē* to encompass all of creation, the entire created order, in such a way that would eventually diminish the lines of distinction between what we mean by "ecumenical" and by "interfaith." It is written in the belief that the ecumenical movement in the next decade should try to seek understanding and relationship with interfaith partners.

Such a development would direct the nature of our ecumenical relationships toward a richer and broader view, one that does not limit *oikumenē* to seeking closer communion among Christian traditions, but one that seeks deep relationships between Islam, Judaism, and Christianity. This is a search for reconciliation toward which Clifton Kirkpatrick has contributed so much.

Chapter 15

The Body Lies Bleeding

Wounds of the Divided Church

JOSEPH D. SMALL

*J*ohn Calvin is remembered as a separatist who rejected the Catholic Church with enflamed rhetoric and bitter invective. There is no doubt that his censure of the late medieval Catholic Church and its practices was pervasive, yet the purpose of his critique was always reform, not separation. Even when he recognized the need for a diversity of churches in different geographical locations, and even when he engaged in sharp theological and ecclesial disputes, he always understood that the restored unity of the church was a gospel imperative.

When the Reformation was still in its early stages, Cardinal Sadoleto wrote a letter to the government and citizens of Geneva, imploring them to return to the Catholic Church. In his letter, Sadoleto contrasted fifteen centuries of Catholic unity with the current division of the church, bemoaning the profusion of differing "sects" spawned by the Reformers: "For already, since these men began, how many sects have torn the Church? sects not agreeing with them, yet disagreeing with each other."[1] A young John Calvin replied to Sadoleto by acknowledging that the most serious of Catholic charges against the Reformers was "that we have attempted to dismember the Spouse of Christ. Were that true," Calvin wrote, "both you and the whole world might regard us as desperate." Though acknowledging the reality of divisions within the church, Calvin denied that sole responsibility lay with the proponents of reformation: "I admit that, on the revival of the gospel, great disputes arose where all was quietness before. But that is unjustly imputed to our [reformers], who, during the whole course of their proceedings, desired nothing more than that religion being revived, the Churches, which discord had scattered and dispersed, might be gathered together into true unity."[2]

As years passed, Calvin became increasingly disturbed by the fragmentation of the church. In a remarkable letter to Archbishop of Canterbury Thomas Cranmer, Calvin agonized, "This other thing also is to be ranked among the chief evils of our time, viz., that the Churches are so divided, that human fellowship is scarcely now in any repute among us. . . . Thus it is that the members of the Church being severed, the body lies bleeding."[3] He also wrote to the Reformed Churches in France about his conviction that a universal council of the church was necessary to put an end to the divisions in Christendom. The hoped-for council should include representatives from the whole church, Calvin wrote, for he was willing to include the Catholic bishops in the council as long as it also incorporated elected persons who desired the reform of the church. He was even open to the possibility that the pope would preside (but not rule) over the council.[4]

Calvin's hopes were not realized. Within a generation the Protestant movement had splintered into distinct branches—Lutheran, Reformed, Anabaptist, and Anglican—that became increasingly distant from, and often hostile to, one another. In turn, these branches splintered repeatedly so that, in our time, thousands of separate churches are strewn across the world. Church divisions are occasionally healed, but most have endured, so that denominationalism is simply "the way things are" for most contemporary Christians. Moreover, there persists a strong impulse to further split the already-divided churches whenever disagreements emerge over doctrines or morals. Division is assumed to be the normal condition of the church, and thus the unity of Christ's church is consigned to a distant future or relegated to empty invisibility.

Calvin would be horrified to see that his attempts to renew the one holy catholic apostolic church resulted in the fragmentation of the churches, and mortified to hear his efforts at reform being used to justify continuous division. Certainly Calvin was not a casual ecumenist. He viewed disagreements among the churches over questions of doctrine and morals as matters of grave significance, which he was not willing to paper over with easy tolerance or institutional compromise. But Calvin's passionate commitment to the unity of the church stands in marked contrast to contemporary satisfaction with denominational proliferation, ready multiplication of church splits, and indifference toward ecumenical efforts to shape meaningful forms of church unity.

For Calvin, unity within a congregation, unity among congregations, unity within regional and national churches, and unity among separated churches— these were all of a piece. Perhaps we can learn from our forebear's plaintive cry: "Oh, were this thought deeply impressed upon our minds, that we are subject to a law which no more permits the children of God to differ among themselves than the kingdom of heaven to be divided. . . . How should we dread every kind of animosity, if we duly reflected that all who separate us from brethren, estrange us from the kingdom of God!"[5]

Yet even our efforts for unity tacitly assume the continuing independence of the churches. We do not lament our multiple levels of separation or yearn for the day when genuine communion in faith, sacraments, and mission will be the reality in our congregations, in our communities, in our countries, among Reformed churches, and throughout the world. Instead, we continue to assume the continuing division of the body of Christ into distinct, separated entities as a characteristic of "the way things are." We settle for conciliar arrangements among institutional churches that remain essentially autonomous. It may take something as striking as Ephraim Radner's rhetoric to awake us to the devitalized condition of our "ecumenical" denominations and their congregations, not to mention the churches that take pride in their separation:

> Consider that the debilitation of the Body of Christ, the encroaching paralysis of its senses, is hardly a reality its members greet with comprehension. . . . Indeed, the most manifest mark of the divided church appears to be its own insensitivity to the symptoms of its condition. No stench reaches its nostrils; no shame cracks its heart.[6]

The Credibility of the Gospel

The actual unity of the church is not merely a matter of missional cooperation, ecclesiastical diplomacy, or even of so-called full-communion agreements. It is a feature of the integrity of the gospel. Jesus prayed,

> As you, Father, are in me and I am in you,
> may they also be in us
> *so that the world may believe that you have sent me.*
> The glory that you have given me I have given them,
> so that they may be one, as we are one.
> I in them and you in me,
> that they may become completely one,
> *so that the world may know that you have sent me*
> *and have loved them even as you have loved me.*
>   (John 17:21–23 versified, stress added)

The desperate need for the visible oneness of the Christian community is not for the sake of the church. Christian unity is for the sake of the world—for the sake of those who do not know that God has sent the Beloved into the world and who do not know that the Father loves them as he loves the Son. Jesus' prayer grows from his sure understanding that the oneness of his community is a reflection of the oneness of the Father and the Son, and thus a visible proclamation that God's new way in the world is known in Jesus Christ. God's way is the way of divine love for the world and human love within the world. Jesus' prayer makes an explicit link between the unity of the church, the world's knowledge that the Father has sent the Son, and the world's assurance that the Father's love for the world is grounded in the mutual love of the Father and the Son.

But the world does not see a unified Christian community. The world sees "Christianity" in a fractured, dizzying, kaleidoscopic image of differentiated church institutions: Orthodox, Catholic, Protestant, and Pentecostal—each separated from the other, and the latter two endlessly subdivided into competing and often hostile church bodies. In the United States, the world sees prominent denominations such as the Episcopal Church, the Presbyterian Church (U.S.A.), and the Southern Baptist Convention internally split by public disputes, while other denominations are characterized by the internal proliferation of competing affinity groups.

What the world sees in North America, and increasingly throughout the world, is an array of churches that look and act like marketplace commodities. Denominations regularly advertise themselves in national media campaigns, differentiating themselves from other churches by targeting niche markets. Congregations engage in local promotions, peddling a full range of religious goods and services. At all levels, churches put themselves forward as the best option for meeting the real and imagined needs of the shrinking number of religion's consumers. These efforts are often called "evangelism," but they have less to do with the good news of salvation in Christ than with the marketing of full-service religious institutions. The churches turn mission away from the world and inward upon themselves, existing mainly to serve the collective needs of their new and old members while competing with one another for market share in a declining demographic. Far from proclaiming the gospel, the churches proclaim themselves, without a hint of discomfort or embarrassment.

Churchly competition, so thoroughly American, simply confirms the world's lurking suspicion that churches care less about seeking and saving the lost than about increased market share, less about love of God and neighbors than about seeking additional adherents, all in order to enhance institutional prominence and finance future expansion. Yet beneath the world's conviction that churches, like other institutions in American society, are in the sales business, and beneath the world's suspicion of churches' motives, lies a deeper and more troubling consequence of the divided church. It is but a short leap from the commodification of the church to the commodification of God. Choosing a church, choosing a religion, choosing a god, leads straight to "I determine what God is."[7] The separated churches support generic American religiosity in its predisposition to shop for a god that meets its needs.

What the world does not see in the all-too-visible disunity of the churches is a sign of the unity of the Father and the Son. Jesus prayed that we might be one *"so that the world may know that you have sent me and have loved them even as you have loved me"* (John 17:23, stress added). We certainly are not one, which obscures the gospel, rendering less accessible to the world the good news that "when the fullness of time had come, God sent his Son, born of a woman, born under the law, in order to redeem those who were [born] under the law, so that we might receive adoption as children" (Gal. 4:4). Bruce Marshall puts the matter starkly: "The credibility of the gospel—of the message that the triune God gives his own eternal life to the world in the missions of the Son and Spirit—depends upon the unity of the church by which that life is exhibited to the world. . . . The unity of the church is a necessary condition for holding the gospel true."[8]

Simply put, the disunity of the church calls into question the believability of the gospel. Thus, Jesus prayed that we may be one so that those outside of the church can know and believe that God loves them, and that God's love for them is tangible in the sending of Jesus Christ to the world. The visible manifestation of this good news should be the character of a Christian community that is united in its belief in the Son of God, Jesus Christ, and in love for one another (1 John 3:23). Perhaps the most basic task of a "missional" church is to strive for the visible unity of the Christian community so that the world may see, know, and believe the gospel.

The recently released report of the American Religious Identification Survey contains the sobering news that between 1990 and 2008 the percentage of Americans who identify themselves as Christian dropped by 10 percent while the percentage of persons who do not identify with any religious faith doubled.[9] Christian claims for the transforming truth of the gospel are drowned out by the clamor of competing religious and nonreligious options. More distressingly, the credibility of Christian claims is undermined by the institutional rivalry of denominations and congregations that are in competition with one another for a share of the dwindling religious market. The unity of the churches is no longer a matter of merely internal ecclesial interest; the unity of the churches is a necessary condition for the proclamation of the gospel in an increasingly indifferent culture.

The Unity We Seek

The ecumenical task of the churches is not to produce a monolithic super-church, but to achieve genuine *communion* in common (not uniform) faith, common (not uniform) worship, and common (not uniform) mission. The unity of genuine communion is not achieved by councils of churches, loose alliances of churches, or even so-called full-communion agreements. Tellingly, churches that have entered into formal agreements of full communion continue to frame theological statements, take moral positions, order ministries, and amend polities without consultation, let alone the concurrence of their sister churches. Mutual responsibility and accountability, so fundamental to *koinōnia*, are pushed aside as churches continue to order their faith and life apart from one another.

Various forms of reconciled diversity, gift-giving, and (less than) full communion are surely preferable to the estranged antagonisms of the past, but they carry with them an illusion of significant unity. Far too often they describe comfortable arrangements of mutual forbearance that permit churches to remain self-contained while feeling better about their continuing separation. The separated churches' confidence in their ecclesial self-sufficiency carries with it practices of institutional autonomy that are masked by a variety of pragmatic cooperative arrangements. Taking comfort in the illusion of unity inhibits the churches' capacity to recognize the reality of their continued separation and dulls them to the pain of division within the body of Christ.

What, then, is to be done? The course is not laid out, but the starting point is known: repentance. From the Groupe des Dombes' *For the Conversion of the Churches*, to the Princeton Proposal's *In One Body through the Cross*, to John Paul II's *Ut Unum Sint*, deep repentance—confession, turning, conversion—has been seen as the necessary starting point for the renewal of the gospel imperative to strive for the unity of Christ's church.

- "Our confessions have to 'make confession,'" says the Groupe des Dombes, "to move forward to admit their limitations and inadequacies, even sins."[10]
- The Princeton Proposal declares that "we must examine our collective consciences and repent of our actions, habits, and sentiments that glory in division."[11]
- John Paul II noted explicitly that "there is an increased sense of the need for repentance: an awareness of certain exclusions which seriously harm fraternal charity, for certain refusals to forgive, of a certain pride, of an unevangelical insistence on condemning 'the other side,' of a disdain born of an unhealthy presumption."[12]

Before we pray "that we may be one," we must acknowledge that we are all complicit in the fragmentation of the church. Without the deep repentance in which the churches acknowledge that they are not whole without the other, and that continuing division is disobedience, broad and deep ecumenical engagement remains a mere option that may or may not be exercised. Yet in a religiously plural world and an increasingly secularized Europe and North America, acquiescence to the continued division and multiplication of churches does more than question the integrity of the churches themselves. The continued shattering of the church, coupled with brazen ecclesial competition, mutes the proclamation of the gospel and weakens the credibility of witness to the way, truth, and life of Christ.

Throughout his ministry, Cliff Kirkpatrick has understood that sustained ecumenical engagement is not an optional activity. As director of Global Mission and then stated clerk of the Presbyterian Church (U.S.A.), and as president of the World Alliance of Reformed Churches, he has been a tireless worker for the unity of the body of Christ. But Cliff understands that while partial ecumenical achievements are good and necessary, they do not resolve the fundamental crisis. The chief evil of Calvin's time remains the chief evil of our day: the church is dismembered, and the body lies bleeding. Working to heal the wounds of the divided church is not only the task of recognized ecumenists like Cliff; it is also the calling of all who are members of the wounded and bloody body of Christ.

Chapter 16

Reflections on Ecumenism
in the Calvin Year

JANE DEMPSEY DOUGLASS

*A*fter a year of celebrating our heritage from John Calvin, it seems appropriate to probe more deeply into the richness of that foundation for our thinking about our ecumenical stance.

Two passages are regularly quoted from Calvin with relation to ecumenical work. One is from the *Institutes*: "Wherever we see the Word of God purely preached and heard, and the sacraments administered according to Christ's institution, there, it is not to be doubted, a church of God exists."[1] The context clearly shows that Calvin intends this definition to be a charitable one that will protect the unity of the church against malicious attempts to divide it.

Many churches of the Reformed tradition have focused on the breadth of definition in this passage to acknowledge with a generous spirit a wide variety of churches as our sister churches in the body of Christ, to which we have obligations.

The other regularly quoted passage comes from a letter to Archbishop Thomas Cranmer of England, where Calvin replies warmly to Cranmer's proposal for a gathering of Christian leaders to further church unity. He considers the division of the churches "among the chief evils of our time . . . Thus is it that the members of the Church being severed, the body lies bleeding. So much does this concern me, that, if I could be of any service, I would not grudge to cross even ten seas, if need be, on account of it."[2] This passage has symbolized Calvin's passion for outreaching hospitality to Christians who have become separated. Calvin saw himself as pastor to a wide international diaspora of Reformed churches, and he reached out through letters and the printed word, not only to Reformed churches but also to those of other traditions. He also made Geneva an international center for theological education and a haven for religious refugees.

In this spirit the world bodies of the World Alliance of Reformed Churches and the Reformed Ecumenical Council over the last century and a quarter have brought together Reformed Christians from across those many seas to express their oneness in personal encounters and in concrete action for mutual support and common witness. Dialogue has also been fostered at the national level, where there may be several Reformed churches not in any active relation to one another or struggling to overcome painful divisions. Reaching out beyond the Reformed family, WARC has actively sponsored bilateral and multilateral dialogues with Christian bodies of all traditions for almost fifty years.

Nonetheless, with respect to the passage quoted from the *Institutes*, we are aware that groups within our churches and other churches with Calvinistic theology have shifted the emphasis to stress emphatically the need for the "purity" of teaching of the faith and sacramental practice before full recognition can be given to a church. So its effect has sometimes been to encourage division and discourage engagement in the ecumenical movement. In recent years the well-publicized growth of "Neo-Calvinism" has given new prominence to conservative evangelical churches that emphasize their Calvinist roots while interpreting Calvin in ways that distance them from mainstream Reformed churches.

Surely one important task confronting the new World Communion of Reformed Churches, whose birth we joyfully celebrate this year after a long period of preparation and waiting, is to reach out still further to Reformed churches not yet drawn into the family of the WCRC and also to others that claim Calvin's theology. Yet that is only the beginning of the task. WCRC must reach beyond the Reformed family, continuing to build relationships with established world confessional bodies while also searching out the less structured Christian movements, which we do not understand as well.

Where in Calvin's thought can one find the wellspring of his passion for Christian unity, which has pressed so many Reformed people into leadership in the ecumenical movement? Why was he so conflicted about the divisions resulting from the very process of reform that he enthusiastically led? It may be helpful to identify three biblical visions of solidarity that Calvin emphasizes again and again and that underlie his desire for unity.

1. The bond of human solidarity, the original solidarity of all humanity created in the image of God, and the common fall of all humanity into sin. Ethical obligations are created by common humanity. Calvin eloquently appeals to the image of God in every human being, however corroded by sin, as a claim to justice. "Therefore, whomever you meet who needs your aid, you have no reason to refuse to help. . . . Say that the person does not deserve

even your least effort for his or her own sake; but the image of God, which recommends the person to you, is worthy of your giving yourself and all your possessions."[3]

2. The bond of solidarity between Christ and fallen humanity. Jesus Christ, the true image of God, took upon himself full humanity, sharing our nature and our life. A common image used by Calvin to express this solidarity is "bone of our bones, flesh of our flesh." Only through such a union of divinity with humanity can the image of God in human beings be restored.

3. The bond of solidarity among believers called into the church by the Holy Spirit. There is one church because there is one body of Christ into which all the baptized are knit together. Speaking of the Lord's Supper, Calvin says:

> We shall benefit very much from the Sacrament if this thought is impressed and engraved upon our minds: that none of the brothers [or sisters] can be injured, despised, rejected, abused or in any way offended by us, without at the same time, injuring, despising, and abusing Christ by the wrongs we do; . . . that we cannot love Christ without loving him in the brothers [and sisters]; that we ought to take the same care of our brothers' [and sisters'] bodies as we take of our own; for they are members of our body; . . . Augustine . . . frequently calls this Sacrament "the bond of love."[4]

From reflection on Calvin's intense preoccupation with human solidarity, some thoughts arise for our future ecumenical agenda.

1. Most modern Protestants have become so accustomed to the idea of church life divided into many parallel streams that Christian division no longer seems scandalous. A task before us is to help our congregations grasp the seriousness of the divisions that still hinder full communion and diminish our witness to the world. An equally important task is encouraging congregations to act together with ecumenical partners on agreement already achieved. Keeping a biblical vision of the one body of Christ vivid in preaching and teaching is essential. Baptisms are an occasion for sermon and liturgy to proclaim one Lord, one faith, one baptism—one church into which we have all been baptized. Celebrations of the Lord's Supper can refocus congregations on the length and breadth of the table spread before them. Regular prayer for other Christians and for Christian unity can also shape our spirituality. Learning to care deeply about the unity of Christ's body, the church, is a matter of spiritual maturation. Our theological seminaries need to be engaged in this learning process.

2. Calvin's vivid description of the bond of love within the body of Christ challenges us. How do we know when we are offending our brothers and sis-

ters if we do not take the trouble to talk honestly with them? How can we be silent about our hungry brothers and sisters across town or around the world if we are to care for their bodies like our own? Our neglect is an offense not only against them, but also against Christ.

Ecumenism is not a purely academic discipline, though wide knowledge of history, theology, and church life is essential. Ecumenism is also a work of love, a process of deep personal engagement with our brothers and sisters to the point where empathy and compassion flow naturally, where offenses— present or historical—can be confessed and forgiven. Really hearing the stories of others may be difficult and painful. Even within our own churches we have to hear the stories of those offended and shut out because of their race or economic status, their gender or gender orientation, or because of power struggles. Race, gender, and gender orientation have also come to be church-dividing issues in the ecumenical world along with traditional issues such as sacramental theology or church governance. Reaching across confessional lines, we have to hear stories of brutal suppression of minority churches, of hurtful stereotypes and misrepresentations, of ignorance and arrogance. But until we hear the stories honestly, we will not truly know how our brothers and sisters have been offended or how we can bring about reconciliation within the one body of Christ.

It is easy to celebrate the variety of cultures within the Reformed or the wider Christian family from afar. When we have to make decisions together at the world level, however, we often have to confront history and the offenses caused by colonialism and contemporary global economic injustice, and we have to understand different ways of thinking theologically and making decisions. In many of our American presbyteries, the world has come to us in the form of congregations of immigrants from many nations. We often offend one another without knowing the pain we cause, because we have not learned how to talk to one another honestly. It is a work of love to find ways to share our wisdom in mutuality. It is a joy to hear the gospel sung beautifully and freshly in a different key and to feel reconciliation in the body of Christ. It is a source of strength and courage—and our proper calling—to stand together for justice in the economy and for the earth, as Reformed people have done in the Accra Confession.

Ecumenical encounters should be carefully organized, and we have created some useful institutions, such as bilateral and multilateral dialogues and councils of churches, that need our continuing support. But encounters also happen in unexpected ways and places. We have to follow the work of the Spirit to identify new arenas where Christians are finding one another, often by working together to meet the needs of the wider community.

3. Our solidarity with all humanity requires us to enter respectfully into dialogue with persons of all faiths and of no faith. The dispersion of many world religions across the globe brings unfamiliar ones to our neighborhoods. We need to learn about them and prove our willingness to work with their followers wherever possible for the common good of our communities. We must stand with them in defense of religious freedom if theirs is challenged, and stand in defense of justice for all.

Chapter 17

The Ecumenical Stance
of the Presbyterian Church (U.S.A.)

The Nature of the Unity We Seek

ANNA CASE-WINTERS

*T*he vision of ecumenism unfolded in the Ecumenical Stance of the Presbyterian Church (U.S.A.)[1] came to its full flowering and particular shape under the leadership of Cliff Kirkpatrick and persons he has encouraged in the work of ecumenism. The statement retrieves and reaffirms our historic commitment to ecumenism and at the same time seeks a faithful response to the new realities distinctive to the contemporary context. It is one of many significant achievements of Cliff's years of service. All who are committed to the pursuit of a more visible unity of the church owe a great debt of gratitude to Cliff Kirkpatrick. He has had a heart for the unity of the church, and his energy and enthusiasm for ecumenism have inspired and prodded us forward all along the way. In my work with the General Assembly Committee on Ecumenical Relations and with the World Alliance of Reformed Churches, I have had the privilege of sitting at many an ecumenical dialogue table. What I know is that when Cliff Kirkpatrick was a part of the workings, things just went better. So often where there were difficulties, differences, and discouragement, it was his calm, reasonable, hopeful, and winsome spirit that helped us to stay at it a while longer until we found a way forward together. At times I felt as if it was the "glue" of his personal graciousness that held us to our seats at the tables of ecumenical dialogue! What a gift he has been to our church—to God be the glory.

This brief contribution will consider some central convictions concerning the nature of the unity of the church as they are embedded in the Stance Statement. My task will be to lift these up for closer examination and elaborate their theological grounding and a few of their implications for the challenges that lie ahead.

The Unity of the Church Is Both the Gift
and the Calling of God

As the closing affirmation of the Ecumenical Stance declares, unity in Christ is "a unity not of our making but a gift designed and revealed by the Maker of us all." Our unity in Christ is a gift of God. Just as we did not create this unity, neither can we destroy it. Even our divisions cannot destroy our unity. What our divisions do is to obscure our unity and hamper our witness. We are at tables of ecumenical dialogue not in order to *create* unity, but because we are already one in Christ and are seeking to make our unity visible by overcoming divisions that contradict it. We believe God calls us to this work. In Jesus' prayer in John 17:1–26, he prayed that we might "all be one . . . so that the world may believe." Thus the unity of the church is both gift and calling.

The Unity of the Church Entails
Our "Doing Difference Differently"

We live in an age that celebrates diversity. A call to unity is often met with a certain amount of caution and suspicion. It raises questions: Whose unity? Unity on what terms? There is some concern that a dominant group may be seeking to assimilate other groups and make their values and practices the universal norm. The call to unity is heard as a call to uniformity, and the submerging of particular identities as differences are to be "overcome." On the contrary, differences are not what must be overcome—rather *divisions* based upon differences.[2] Our differences may well be recognized and celebrated—even treated as gifts we have to offer to one another. In the work of ecumenism, many of us can testify to the reality of the giving and receiving of gifts as we engage in "mutual affirmation and admonition."

The apostle Paul uses the image of the church as the "body of Christ" (Rom. 12; 1 Cor. 12). It is a metaphor that conveys well the nature of our diverse unity. There are many members, diverse gifts, and different forms of ministry, and yet there is one body. As in a body that is a living organic whole, so also we in the church are all connected, joined together, belonging to one another. Practices that sever members do injury to the body. In this powerful image we have at one and the same time an embrace of difference and a rejection of division. The call to unity in the church is a call to do difference differently.

The Unity of the Church Is Essential
to Its Very Being as Church

Traditional marks of the church begin with unity. The Nicene Creed boldly confesses belief in "one holy catholic and apostolic church." Unity is essential, not optional. Theologian Peter Hodgson argues that unity is part of the *fundamental logic* of Christian faith. We are oriented toward one single central figure and event—Jesus Christ and God's redemptive activity in him.[3] Whatever our differences, our shared orientation toward Christ necessarily draws us into unity with one another. What is drawn together is presumed to be (and to remain) genuinely different. The differences, however—such as those between Jew and Greek, male and female, slave and free (Gal. 3:28)— no longer serve as grounds for alienation, division, exclusion, or oppression. Because of our unity in Christ, we have become a "transfigured" community, in which is "fragmentarily actualized a universal reconciling love that liberates from sin and death and alienation and oppression."[4] This kind of unity is essential to what it means to be church.

The Unity of the Church Is Global
in Its Proportions

The vision statement quotes the Second Helvetic Confession's recognition that the one church is *universal* (catholic), "scattered through all parts of the world and extended unto all times, and is not limited to any times or places."[5] The global proportions of the work for unity are pulling the ecumenical movement in new directions that will imply some changes for us. The vision statement recognizes that in global ecumenism today, the "flow of influence is no longer from north to south or even from west to east, but from every part of the world to every other part of the world." The landscape has truly changed.

There was a time when Europe and North America dominated the dialogues: setting the ecumenical table, deciding who would be invited and what would be discussed. Recent history has seen something of a general decline in mainline denominations in Europe and North America, whereas many of the former "mission churches" are growing and vital. Churches in these regions do not necessarily conform to the patterns and prescriptions of their "parent" churches. Inherited denominational distinctions do not apply in the same way. New, distinctive, and thoroughly enculturated ways of being church are emerging. Signals are being sent of weariness with sixteenth-century controversies and readiness to get on with another set of questions. A passing over and passing away of some old models of ecumenism may be an implication of the global proportions of ecumenical work in the contemporary context. Surely a bigger table and some new seating arrangements are implied for global ecumenism in the twenty-first century.

The Unity of the Church Is Lived Out in Its Shared Calling to Work for Justice

The Ecumenical Stance invites us to sustained and serious engagement with the Accra Confession of the World Alliance of Reformed Churches, Covenanting for Justice in the Economy and the Earth. It is a confession that reminds us that the Greek root *oikos*—found in *ecu*menism, *eco*logy, and *eco*nomy—means "household." The whole creation and the whole human family together are God's "household," and it is God's intention that we may all "have life, and have it abundantly" (John 10:10). The question before us, then, is how we may live our lives together in just and sustainable patterns that allow for the flourishing of all.

The Unity of the Church Is Lived Out in Its Shared Calling to Work for Peace

The Ecumenical Stance also calls us to a "covenanting for peacemaking in a war-torn world." A central text for this calling is 2 Corinthians 5:19: "In Christ God was *reconciling the world* to himself . . . and entrusting the message of reconciliation to us" (stress added). The worldwide dimension of our calling to a ministry of reconciliation is clear in the text. Yet how effective can we be in this work that has been entrusted to us if we cannot even be reconciled among ourselves? When we view the hostilities and divisions in the life and history of the church, we may be tempted to wonder whether God has made a mistake in entrusting such work to us. Seeking reconciliation—both in the church and in the world that God so loves—is nevertheless implied in the unity that is God's gift and God's calling to us. When "we are in our right mind" (2 Cor. 5:13), in the mind of Christ, we may become instruments in God's work of reconciliation.

The Unity of the Church Entails Acting Together

The Ecumenical Stance paper urges that "Christians should take united action whenever they find this possible." This is from the Lund Principle, which takes its name from the World Council of Churches' Faith and Order Conference held in Lund, Sweden, in 1952, in which participants agreed that churches should "act together in all matters except those in which deep differences of conviction compel them to act separately."[6] In matters of such large scope as working for justice and peace in the wider world, the wisdom of this principle comes into sharper focus. We can hardly have much impact unless we do work together.

An extension of this principle may imply intentional partnerships with persons of other faith traditions. As the vision statement reminds us, "We are called to join with all those willing to work for the healing of the whole earth and the whole human family." We have already been involved in significant interfaith dialogue, seeking to better understand the working of God's Spirit in persons of other faiths. We have eagerly shared the good news we have received in Jesus Christ even as we have opened ourselves to hearing the good news that persons of other faiths may share with us. The urgency of these dialogues becomes all the more clear when we "covenant for peacemaking" because religious conflict itself has been a major source of discord and violence in our world today. Religious language (i.e., good and evil) is often enlisted in the cause of war. Jonathan Swift's acid observation is to the point: we have "just enough religion to make us hate one another but not enough to make us love one another."[7] The great faiths working together have the potential—too little realized—of becoming a force for peace and for the justice upon which peace ultimately depends.

In closing, I commend a close consideration of the Ecumenical Stance of the Presbyterian Church (U.S.A.). It illumines a pathway forward in our quest to make the unity of the church more visible. This undertaking is both complicated and urgent for the church today. It is not up to us to bring it about, for this unity is God's gift to us. Neither is it allowable for us to give up on its full visibility, for this unity is God's calling to us.

Chapter 18

Christian Unity in the 21st Century

EUGENE TURNER

I was born during the twentieth century and have lived about ten years into the twenty-first, and I have dedicated much of my professional life to the search for Christian unity. Hence, I am encouraged to think that the twenty-first century may be ushering in a new day and a new time for my own church, if not for all churches, at least those that can hear the Gospel of John's call for unity among the followers of Christ. Yes, we have been serious before, but Christian unity is still elusive. It is a new century! It is a novel religious world! Clifton Kirkpatrick, a product of the same era, one who has climbed the same ecumenical hills and dwelled in the same ecumenical valleys as I, is appropriately honored in these pages. This essay explores how the Spirit is informing my thinking on Christian unity today. I pray that I am speaking on behalf of others and not only for myself.

A Personal Link to the Twentieth-Century
Christian Unity Movement

My Christian life began during the 1950s, when I was eight years old and was baptized by a Baptist congregation in Sandersville, Georgia. I was nurtured in the faith by another Baptist congregation in Macon, Georgia, where I grew up. My knowledge of the church of Christ did not extend beyond these early childhood experiences. Observing what to me was the hypocrisy of churches in race relations in the culture of my early Christian environment, I claimed agnosticism early on and into college. During these years Christian-unity language was null and void in my Christian nurture. My experience is probably not that different from others of my age. The social context of this experience in Georgia, where racial segregation was total and state ordered, began to shape my sense of the church and world. If the churches wanted to defy this relational barrier, they could not. Discussing Christian unity in this context was nonsensical.

Here is an example that my fellow chorus members experienced as an indicator of the kind of hypocrisy we endured. I recall entering from the back of a church with my high school chorus, to sing before a white congregation in Macon, Georgia. The chorus director was told that we could not process from the front of the sanctuary because some in the congregation did not want black students entering the front of the church building.

The pietistic Presbyterian Church that I found on the college campus in 1953 became my first exposure to a wider view of the Christian faith with which I found favor. It had vespers at least once a week and worship on Sunday, and for some, even Sunday school. Except in worship liturgy, Christian unity discussions were missing. During the many vespers and services of worship, prayer for the unity of the church, if present at all, was indeed subtle.

From my early childhood I knew of the separation of southern white and black people along racial lines, but I did not know the extent of this separation along Christian and religious lines. It was through college interfaith dialogues focused on race relations that I learned of religious and faith divisions.

I contend that my experience was rather typical. Persons of my age and older were not exposed to Christian-unity thinking in their Christian nurture. It should not be a surprise that the churches did not talk officially and publicly about Christian unity until 1942, when the Presbyterians and the Episcopalians drafted a proposal for deeper dialogue, which was, however, stopped by the Episcopal Church's rejection of the proposal. There was progress in the 1960s, when Dr. Eugene Carson Blake of the United Presbyterian Church (U.S.A.) and Bishop James A. Pike of the Protestant Episcopal Church in America introduced the concept of COCU, the Consultation on Church Union. I was a young seminarian at the time. This was the first time all of the United States, secular and religious, became animated over church unity.

On the campus of Knoxville College in Tennessee, I was exposed to interfaith dialogue in the interest of better race relations. These discussions were between Jews and African Americans, who shared some of the same pain of the separation of races in Tennessee. Some white students volunteered to be part of the deliberations. No intentional word was mentioned about the significance of the two faiths' traditions. Little did I know the importance of these discussions for shaping my ecumenical and interfaith understanding of my calling to the Christian ministry.

This experience was a fortuitous nurturing in understanding the breadth of the Christian Church. It is characteristic of how the Christian Church has dealt with the ecumenical nurturing of its young followers. This is unfortunate. If we were serious about changing the way the churches seek Christian unity, a more purposeful approach of preparing its members for leadership in Christian unity would be more useful.

I conclude this section with a reflection from Michael Kinnamon's book *Truth and Community*:

> I am convinced that with God, it is possible—indeed, essential—for the church to reject the pretensions of Caesar while still humbly acknowledging that its hold on truth is not absolute. It is possible—essential—for the church to be an inclusive community of diverse groups—Protestant, Catholic, and Orthodox, black and white, liberal and conservative, Russian and American, male and female—while still drawing firm lines against apartheid and other examples of lovelessness, or against allegiance to lesser gods. The fact that our churches so often split these concerns—parochialism and idolatry, diversity and truth—indicates how little the ecumenical vision is understood. And, without a proper understanding, it is no wonder that ecumenism is low on many of the churches' lists of priorities, something they pay lip service to while their passion lies elsewhere.[1]

In this brief essay, we cannot fully address the history of confessional and Reformed church relations in the United States. The topic is mentioned here to acknowledge that these reflections are informed by that history. Already noted above, the written ecumenical history of the Protestant and Reformed churches is fairly recent. Clifton Kirkpatrick and I have had similar experiences in our ecumenical nurture, ecclesially and environmentally, since he grew up in Texas and I in Georgia. We shared a working relationship in ecumenical ministry in the Presbyterian Church (U.S.A.) as well.

The Rise of the Permanence of Other World Religions

For too long, Christian churches have behaved as if they were the only major religion alive and active in the world. For too long they have seemed to believe that all the people of the world are potential members of their churches. Due to the rise of other major religions of the world, Christianity is confronted with unity issues it could not have perceived a few decades ago. The Christian church movement gives the impression that within it are multireligions. The real and perceived division in the Christian churches is a serious detriment to its missional, theological, ecclesial, and confessional witness in the world.

The issue is this: How can and should Christian leaders justify church division? It may appear to be an engaging activity today. But tomorrow it could be the cause of its failure to witness in the world. The secularists and the seekers are showing an interest in other religions, some because they do not find a demanding difference among them, although the churches understand the differences. Our church divisions are more difficult to explain. What is the explanation for the separation of multiple church bodies when they adhere to the one Christ, with quite similar doctrine? New Protestant assemblages evolving in the U.S. culture select not to align themselves with any mainline U.S. denomination. Most of these churches have decided that the ecclesial grouping of congregations into what we commonly call denominations is viewed as unessential to the definition of the church. An objective study and analysis of why the megachurches have decided not to connect with mainline denominations in the United States is needed to determine if this behavior represents a new trend.

God gave Christ to the world as Savior. John 3:16 tells us that: "For God so loved the world that he gave his only Son, so that everyone who believes in him may not perish but may have eternal life." It is not clear how the church interprets this great biblical proclamation today. It was once the basis for claiming the world as the stage for Christian evangelism. If the churches were more unified, our message of God's salvation in Jesus Christ would be less diffused.

Christian Churches in the Twenty-first Century

Some confessional and Reformed churches are already on a path toward unity and should be challenged to move to organic union. We observe the example of the Evangelical Lutheran Church in America, the Reformed Church in America, the United Church of Christ, and the Presbyterian Church (U.S.A.). Clifton Kirkpatrick was a bold advocate for the adoption of a Formula of Agreement, placing these churches in full communion with one another. This is a noble accomplishment, a witness of the one church of Christ, though it is a small grouping of churches within a global church perspective.

What are the claims for these churches remaining separated? They share a common understanding of the Scriptures. They claim a oneness in ministry and are theologically in accord with one another. All are confessional, a major commonality of the confessional and Reformed churches. How does one rationalize these churches remaining separated? If they were to form a union, it would be a masterful testimony that the rest of the Christian world would not ignore. A Common Calling states:

The Lutheran and Reformed churches engaged in the present conversations share a common commitment to the authority of Scripture for the faith and life of their communities. They also acknowledge the importance of the ancient creeds and Reformation confessions in providing the essential context within which the contemporary faith of the church is confessed. Each community explicitly states the nature of its confessional commitment in its official documents, and all require a confessional commitment of its ordinands. The language concerning this confessional commitment is diverse. Nonetheless, some common patterns can be discerned within our traditions regarding the authority of confessional writings.[2]

Whether one is thinking theologically, biblically, ecclesially, or ministerially, there is no compelling argument for these churches not forming a union. I am not the first to say this. I state this with all the compassion and hope that a single voice can give.

Chapter 19

Unity: Gift and Demand

*T*he Scriptures are clear that God's intention for the created world is unity, order. The creation narratives in Genesis establish this theme at the very beginning: God addressed the primeval chaos with the creative word, and order came into being and prevailed. The history of the people of God records the repeated gift of order and unity by the Creator. Beginning with the call to Abraham and Sarah and Moses and the prophets, God gave order and unity down through the years.

The theme continues in the Second Testament with the life and teaching of Jesus, as expressed most eloquently in his high-priestly prayer (John 17), in the letters of Paul with, for example, his metaphor of the body and its unity (1 Cor. 12), to the book of Revelation and the vision of the new Jerusalem.

But as we well know, that intended order and unity were quickly and continuously disrupted and ignored by all the generations since the creation. Virtually every page of history, both secular history and church history, contains stories of conflict, abuse, disorder, and disunity. And sometimes secular history gets tangled up in the history of the church.

At the Sixth Assembly of the World Council of Churches (1983) in Vancouver, Canada, Lyndon LaRouche and some of his followers, who tended to see a Communist conspiracy in the most unlikely places, were present and passing out anticommunist literature. They set up a table with a sign that read, "The KGB is an agent of the Russian Orthodox Church. Their intention is to remove the *filioque* clause from the creed." Reading that absurd declaration prompted me to do some research on *filioque*.

In the Nicene Creed the words about the Holy Spirit include the phrase, "who proceedeth from the Father and the Son." The words "and the Son," *filioque*, were not in the original text of the creed of Nicaea (325 CE). They

105

were apparently first inserted at the Council of Toledo in Spain, where "newly converted Goths were required to sign the creed with the addition." The debate was said to be about the interpretation of the Trinity. It was between the churches of the East, centered around Constantinople, that vigorously opposed its use because it seemed to denigrate the position and person of the Holy Spirit; and the churches of the West, centered around Rome, that sought to amend the creed. But the fact that Charlemagne, never remembered for his theological acumen, became involved in the debate in 809 CE indicates that the issue was not simply theological but was political as well, part of the struggle between the Ottoman Empire and the Roman Empire. *Filioque* became a principal cause of the first major split in the church, with the Byzantine churches and the Western churches excommunicating each other in 1054.

More recently there have been further developments relating to *filioque*. The Lambeth Convention of Anglican bishops, meeting some forty years ago and building on their bilateral dialogues with the Orthodox, recommended that the Anglican churches around the world make the *filioque* clause optional when the Nicene Creed is said. And I was told by a Roman Catholic priest that Pope John Paul II omitted the phrase as he said the creed with a leader of the Orthodox churches. The church-dividing issue had become no issue, though the division it caused persists.

An amusing sidebar: When the new *Presbyterian Hymnal* was published in 1990, I noted that in the ecumenical version of the Nicene Creed, the text indicated that "and the Son" was optional. When I pointed that out to the editor, his face fell and he said, "That's a typographical error. The PC(USA) has never made an official statement to that effect, so we are not authorized to indicate in the text that *filioque* is optional."

There have been many other examples of church-dividing situations over issues that seemed at the time to be worth splitting the church over, but which came later to be considered insignificant and certainly not worth the pain and division the issue originally caused.

As people all over the world, including, surprisingly, non-Christians in China, celebrate the 500th anniversary of the birth of John Calvin, it is important to remember his passion for the unity of the church. Writing to the Archbishop of Canterbury, Calvin said, "This other thing also is to be ranked among the chief evils of our time, viz., that the churches are so divided, that human fellowship is scarcely now in any repute among us. . . . Thus it is that the members of the church being severed, the body lies bleeding. So much does this concern me, that, could I be of any service, I would not grudge to cross even ten seas, if need were, on account of it."[1] Yet in spite of Calvin's passionate concern for the unity of the church, Clifton Kirkpatrick, president of the World Alliance of Reformed Churches, reports that there are more splits and divisions among Reformed Christians, theological descendants of Calvin, than in any other theological tradition.

The toughest church-dividing issue, at least for Americans, is the issue of race. The African Methodist Episcopal Church, for example, was started in 1787 when, as the Yearbook of American and Canadian Churches says, "persons in St. George's Methodist Episcopal Church (in Philadelphia) withdrew as a protest against color [racial] segregation." On October 25, 2009, more than two hundred years after that split, the two congregations, St. George's Methodist Episcopal Church and Mother Bethel African Methodist Episcopal Church, worshipped together for the first time: a gift of the Spirit in view of the famous quote from Dr. Martin Luther King Jr. that Sunday morning is the most segregated time in America.[2] And so it continues to be. The African Methodist Episcopal (AME) Church together with two other predominantly African American churches, the African Methodist Episcopal Zion (AMEZ) Church and the Christian Methodist Episcopal Church, worked hard in the Consultation on Church Union (COCU) with the five predominantly white denominations during the forty years of COCU's life, trying to find ways to overcome the church-dividing issues, including the issue of racial justice. Commitments were made all around, but as COCU became Churches Uniting in Christ (CUIC), the struggles of the churches dealing with race and racial justice, in spite of good intentions to the contrary, gradually lost their focus, with the result that the AME and the AMEZ churches have essentially withdrawn from CUIC.

Now, in light of the intention of the Creator and God's gift of order and unity on the one hand, and the sad history of the church (to say nothing about secular history) that has more often split than come together, what are we to do? That's where the demand comes in. Children of God have an obligation to work and pray for unity and order. It is not an elective. It is not just the work of specialists. It is not just on the agenda of the World Alliance of Reformed Churches, the World Council of Churches, or similar organizations. It is the task of all God's children.

One course of action is to pray for unity. The Week of Prayer for Christian Unity was started in 1908 by Rev. Paul Wattson and Mother Lurana White, who were also founders of the Franciscan Society of the Atonement. They set the time for the week between the Feasts of St. Peter and St. Paul, eight days, January 18–25. Now Christians all around the world spend those eight days in special prayer for unity.

At my place of ministry in Japan in 1968, shortly after the Second Vatican Council, I received a notice about the Week of Prayer from the Presbyterian

Mission Board. With some hesitation, I went to see the local Roman Catholic priest to ask if there was anything that we could do together. That very day he had received from his mission order the same material that I had received. We hastily made some plans for the Week and were amazed at the positive response. Roman Catholic and Protestant Christians found each other and were strengthened and encouraged.

A joint committee of the World Council of Churches and the Vatican recommends themes for the Week of Prayer and suggests places in the world where the theme can be further developed. For 2009, an ecumenical group in South Korea developed the theme by using as the text Ezekiel 37:15–28, where God spoke to Ezekiel and said, "They will become one in my hand; . . . they will be my people, and I will be their GOD" (23:19, 23 TNIV).

This essay is not the appropriate place to give a detailed history of the modern ecumenical movement that began, some say, with the formation of the World Alliance of Reformed Churches in 1877 and the World Missionary Conference in 1910. Suffice it here to say that the movement went on from there to include such critically important events and efforts as the formation of the World Council of Churches in 1948, the National Council of Churches in 1950, the work of the Consultation on Church Union that began in 1962 and continued for forty years, culminating in the formation of Churches Uniting in Christ. The Second Vatican Council (1962–65) opened the windows of the Roman Catholic Church in a multitude of ways. Many bilateral dialogues continue to bring understanding and mutual respect to churches. The movement continues.

For example, in 1975 the Presbyterian Church U.S., the so-called Southern Presbyterian Church, held an ecumenical consultation to seek answers to several questions: What does the Lord of the church require of the PCUS today? How do we Presbyterians get from where we are to where we ought to be? Coming together were more than a hundred participants, including all the Southern Presbyterian delegates to ecumenical agencies, as well as representatives from the General Executive Board of the PCUS, the regional synods and various caucuses. At least 20 percent of the participants were from other denominations. There were sages—for example, Francis Pickens Miller, a pre–World War II executive of the World Student Christian Federation—and seminary students and other young ecumenists among the participants, including Clifton Kirkpatrick, who was then serving as the director of the Houston Metropolitan Ministries.

The first and major recommendation of that consultation was this: "The Biblical imperative of visible unity places important and urgent demands upon the PCUS. While we long and pray for Christian Unity, we must also work for it. Therefore the PCUS should take action to deepen its involvement in the ecumenical life and witness of Christ's Church." The work of that consultation with that widely representative group of participants affected each participant in different ways, surely. But I believe it is fair to say that the influence of that gathering was a significant gift of the old Southern Presbyterian Church to the whole ecumenical church around the world.

The demand of the theme continues. God's gift of unity is still in need of demonstration. So we keep on working and praying for the unity of the church, grateful to God always for leaders who will help us all respond more faithfully to God's imperative. Thanks be to God.

Chapter 20

Political Advocacy as a Dimension of Ecumenism

MICHAEL KINNAMON

*I*t is a pleasure to offer these brief reflections as a tribute to Cliff Kirkpatrick and his ministry in the ecumenical church. A crucial part of Cliff's ecumenical witness has been advocacy, work for social transformation through political engagement, carried out through councils of churches. My own experience, as the former chairperson of the National Council of Churches' Justice and Advocacy Commission, and now as the NCC's General Secretary, is that advocacy is most profound when it maintains certain tensions, four of which I discuss in this essay.

One of the things I have so appreciated about Cliff is his insistence that common witness to Christ, theological dialogue aimed at unity in the body of Christ, and advocacy for justice in Christ's name are complementary responses to the gospel and thus belong together in the one ecumenical movement. My focus on a single strand of ecumenism must be seen as part of this broader effort if it is true to Cliff's own vision.

The *first tension* I want to name is the need, on the one hand, for *focused* attention on particular advocacy priorities and the need, on the other hand, for advocacy that *integrates* multiple themes, that sees our particular problems within a wider context. In 2009, I spoke at Ecumenical Advocacy Days, an annual event in Washington, DC, on the need for support of quality public education through revision of "No Child Left Behind" legislation. But certainly we cannot simply focus on education alone since part of the problem is inequitable funding based on patterns of race and class. Education needs priority attention, but it cannot be dealt with as an isolated issue.

In recent years, racial justice has been part of the NCC's broader agenda as, for example, in the work of our Special Commission on the Just Rebuilding of the Gulf Coast, which brings together concern for poverty, racism, and environmental destruction in the aftermath of Hurricane Katrina. At our General Assembly last November (2008), the churches affirmed that such an integrated approach is vital, but not sufficient. Racism also demands specific focus, lest we think that the problem is somehow behind us with the election of President Obama.

Since becoming general secretary, I have come to appreciate the need to be very specific in advocacy efforts (e.g., in my proposals to the Israeli ambassador about changing Israeli policy regarding residency permits in Jerusalem and the West Bank), while at the same time fulfilling the need to name broad basic Christian values that potentially refocus public discussion (about which I will say more in a moment). Much of our advocacy work at the NCC, however, falls somewhere in between: not specific enough to get as much done as we would like, and not radical enough to lift up the countercultural voice of Scripture.

A related dilemma is that the NCC has often dissipated its energy and resources on an almost endless list of causes, in part because our members have different priorities. If I meet with the Mar Thoma Church, it is persecution in India. If I meet with the Philadelphia Yearly Meeting, it is handguns in our cities. How are we to take seriously the priorities of our very diverse members and, at the same time, stay focused on the overriding issues of the day? These are things they do not teach us in general secretary school! That is the first tension: focus and integration.

The *second tension* has to do with the need to respond with appropriate urgency to crises of the moment *and* the equally urgent need for long-term formation so that our advocacy grows from our very identity as religious communities. In the United States, in my experience, our churches seem to discover issues with an evangelical zeal, but often retain only short-term interest because they are missing long-term formation.

A Christian advocate who powerfully makes this case is Audrey Chapman, former executive of the United Church of Christ Board for World Ministries, in her book *Faith, Power, and Politics.* "In the absence of shared understandings about identity and vocation," she writes, "political ministry tends to be unfocused and diffuse, lacking explicit theological grounding and sustained membership support and involvement. Political witness tends to become a specialized mission activity undertaken primarily by national agencies . . . on behalf of the denominations, rather than an expression of the community's faith journey." And this leads to a familiar form of hypocrisy whereby what we preach to the world (what we advocate) is not exemplified in our own structures and lifestyles—thereby undercutting the impact of our advocacy. Things like climate change will not wait for long-term education, but surely such education must accompany our efforts and immediate response.

Perhaps this is a good place to name other factors that have, as I see it, diminished the public witness of many of our churches. I will use my own denomination, the Disciples of Christ, as an example.

1. Faced with declining numbers and resources, leaders within the Disciples fear that controversy will further weaken the church. In response, we have, since the mid-1990s, eliminated virtually all national staff positions responsible for social justice ministries and are on the verge of eliminating General Assembly resolutions dealing with contemporary issues.

2. Within the Disciples, as in other mainline churches, there is an evident gap between the commitment of at least some leaders and many local church members. As a result, our assemblies will sometimes offer prophetic witness only to discover that the initiatives lack the broad support needed for church-wide action. That is one reason people have argued for the elimination of resolutions. They too often have been feel-good pronouncements that involve little serious cost or effort.

3. Polarization within the church on issues of social concern, and inability to deal constructively with conflict—this situation means that advocacy is increasingly confined to special interest groups that can be ignored by the rest of the body. I belong to the Disciples Peace Fellowship; but as I keep saying to whomever will listen, the church should not *have* a peace fellowship; it should *be* a peace fellowship.

4. And to return to my basic point, the Disciples have shown little capacity for integrating social witness with worship, pastoral care, stewardship, or the other things the church does and is. In the words of theologian Lew Mudge, "There seems little connection in the minds of church members between the moral convictions to which they bear witness and the nature of the ecclesial community in which these convictions are nurtured"—which means that peace and justice can be relegated to one corner of the church.

The *third tension* I have in mind, and the one I have paid most attention to since becoming general secretary, is nicely set forth in a much-neglected book from 2006, *Beyond Idealism: A Way Ahead for Ecumenical Social Ethics*. In it the authors argue for a perspective that they call "hopeful realism," realistic assessment of our social situation coupled with a willingness to imagine alternative realities. On the one hand, they argue that ecumenical councils have often responded to war, discrimination or environmental destruction with idealized slogans and utopian pronouncements. On the other hand, the NCC in particular has often been reactive to the world's agenda, promoting reforms that, while important, leave the underlying status quo basically untouched. This needs to be said carefully: The NCC leaders have no intention to stop pushing for raises in the minimum wage or calling for more recycling or prompting a reduction in U.S. military spending. But these are ways of tweaking the system and stop short of a truly prophetic witness that engenders hope for a different way of living in human society.

Another person who argues this case is Gary Dorrien, a professor at Union Theological Seminary in New York City. Without a social vision of a Good Society that transcends the prevailing order, he contends, Christian ethics will remain captive to that order, and social Christianity will restrict itself to marginal reforms. I also like the way Chapman puts it: "Our churches seem limited to recommending incremental policy changes that differ little from secular political actions." What is often missing, in her words, "is a compelling religious vision, a sense of the 'now' and the 'not yet' of God's [reign] that challenges and opposes the injustices of the dominant reality by invoking God's peace and justice."

Hopeful realism. *We* cannot eradicate evil. The conceit of such utopianism has itself been the fuel of countless tyrannies. But we also must not allow those responsible for present systems of injustice to define what is possible, because we are followers of God, whose promise is not just for another world but also for *this* world made other.

At the meeting of the NCC's Governing Board last September, our agenda included such things as immigration reform and Christian-Muslim relations. These specific issues are of great importance, and we had proposals for dealing with them. But as I suggested to our board, the underlying problem is the fearfulness of the culture, a fearfulness likely to be exacerbated by the then-impending economic crisis, which turns neighbor against neighbor. Our task as churches, I suggested, is not only to promote legislation and set up dialogues, but also to preach the faith in a way that confronts head-on this culture of fear.

The final tension I want to mention is the dialectic, familiar to our faith communities, of God's initiative and our human response. Much discussion about advocacy emphasizes what we accomplish, and human effort is obviously essential. But seen through a faith perspective, such effort is understood as response to what God has done, is doing, and will do, as participation in God's mission. Getting this theological point straight, in my experience, has very practical benefits; it is a check against self-righteousness. It is a spur to working with others. It is the foundation for deep hopefulness. And it is a reminder to ground all that we do in study of our sacred texts and in prayer. One of the things that has undermined the National Council's social witness in recent years is inadequate theological and biblical foundation, which is usually a sign that we are pushing an ideological agenda rather than opening ourselves to genuine wrestling with our faith heritage.

I will end by noting that councils of churches are both instruments of the churches and of the ecumenical movement. It is not my job as general secretary to press an advocacy agenda in the members; but it is precisely my job to push them when they cling to marks of division or bear only tepid witness to affirmations they have made together with regard to justice and peace. Though Cliff was obviously the head of a member church, he always affirmed this role for conciliar leaders; for this, and so many things, I am deeply grateful.

Chapter 21

The Ecumenical Significance of the World Communion of Reformed Churches

WESLEY GRANBERG-MICHAELSON

*T*he founding of the World Communion of Reformed Churches, to be formalized in June 2010, has far more ecumenical significance than has been commonly recognized. The division between the World Alliance of Reformed Churches and the Reformed Ecumenical Council has mirrored the global walls of separation in the Christian community that became institutionalized following World War II. In founding the WCRC, the Reformed community is taking a pioneering ecumenical initiative that reflects our convictions about belonging to the one church of Jesus Christ. Cliff Kirkpatrick, as president of the WARC, has played a major leadership role in this process.

Although there were particular dynamics around the histories of WARC and REC, together they fit the broader and lamentable global pattern of divided ecumenical trajectories. One trajectory emerged with the establishment of major ecumenical bodies such as the World Council of Churches, formed in 1948, and the National Council of Churches, formed in the United States in 1950. Regional ecumenical bodies began to develop, and national councils of churches soon multiplied across the globe. All this has created the impressive and far-reaching "ecumenical infrastructure" now present throughout the world; it has offered the possibility and challenge of conciliar fellowship to hundreds of denominations and millions of Christians throughout the world.

But from the beginning of the ecumenical movement, other churches counteracted with a different trajectory. Theologically, evangelical Christians were deeply suspicious of these emerging ecumenical organizations and began to define their own identity in opposition to them. Thus the World Evangelical Fellowship was established in 1951 (now called the World Evangelical Alliance), gathering evangelical churches into a global association that was an alternative to the World Council of Churches. In the United States, likewise, the National Association of Evangelicals was formed in 1942 and soon afterward adopted a provision in its constitution that no denomination could be a member of the NAE if it was a member of the National Council of Churches. Throughout the globe, evangelical associations and networks emerged that, for the most part, separated themselves from the ecumenical movement expressed through the World Council of Churches and the global "ecumenical infrastructure."

This is the broader context in which the WARC and the REC functioned and established their identities. We do observe the differences that apply to Christian world communions in their histories and their goals. Yet WARC and REC came to reflect the ecumenical/evangelical polarity that has come to dominate postwar world Christianity. The fact that WARC's offices have been located in Geneva at the Ecumenical Center, and that it has cooperated closely with a broader ecumenical agenda animated by the WCC, emphasizes this identity. Meanwhile, the REC's offices most recently have been in Grand Rapids, Michigan, and many of its member churches are affiliated with the World Evangelical Alliance or national evangelical associations.

Thus the creation of the World Communion of Reformed Churches carries a significance for world Christianity that reaches far beyond the Reformed community. It marks the first time in modern history that two global Christian organizations whose identities were nurtured on opposite sides of the ecumenical/evangelical divide have come together into an actual structural union. The emergence of WCRC is a Reformed witness and declaration to the global church that the evangelical/ecumenical divide can and must be bridged.

All this also comes against the backdrop of the shift in Christianity's global center of gravity from the North to the South. In many ways the polarity between evangelical and ecumenical churches originated in the northern and western hemispheres, and was exported southward and eastward. As one African Christian leader once explained to me, when describing the conflict between ecumenical and evangelical relief and development agencies, "When two elephants fight, our grass gets trampled."

The realities of world Christianity are dramatically changing. The Christian population in Africa, only a few million at the beginning of the twentieth century, now includes over 360 million people, and is projected to grow to 633 million by 2025. By that same time, 640 million Christians would be in Latin America, and 460 million in Asia.[1] The social and economic context of the church within these regions makes the rigid dichotomies of Christianity in the West even less relevant and viable.

New opportunities for fellowship, cooperation, and witness between evangelical and ecumenical expressions of the church are being created as a result of these trends. The impressive receptivity toward the Global Christian Forum, for example, illustrates these possibilities. The World Communion of Reformed Churches will mark a significant step as an example of how organizational divisions that have plagued the global church in the modern postwar era can finally be overcome.

PART 4

For Such a Time as This

*New Directions in Ecumenism
and Mission*

Chapter 22

World Communion Sunday 2020

*R*everend Samantha checks the computer one more time. The link seems to be working, and the projector is burning brightly on the large screen. It is World Communion Sunday, a very special day in the life of First Church in Middletown. Unexpected celebrations could happen as they have in the past.

First Middletown has a relationship with a congregation in Kisumu, Kenya, that has been built on the exchanges of mission trips between the two congregations. The visits by the Kenyans have attracted Kenyans living in Middletown to become members of First Church. The visit by the Middletown members in Kenya has attracted English-speaking Kenyans to the Kisumu congregation.

Rev. Samantha takes a moment to recall how this special day came about. While in seminary twelve years ago, she spent a week at the ecumenical monastery in Taizé, France. There she met the Reverend Wangari Muraya, a young pastor in Kenya. They spent the week in the same working group, cleaning the chapel after morning prayer.

Over lunch, as the working group members were getting to know one another, they began discussing all of the global crises going on in the world and how they felt people in their countries perceived the causes. Samantha was shocked by how differently people interpreted the news. A young man from Scotland commented, "I feel so cynical. It is so easy to talk about the things that frustrate or frighten us, but what about the things that give us hope?"

Rev. Wangari explained what was happening in her country that week. "Just yesterday," she said, "Kenyan president Mwai Kibaki unveiled a new organizational plan for the government, a plan based on power sharing. His

Coauthored with his daughter, Rachel.

political rival will take the post of prime minister. This long-awaited compromise will hopefully end the political crisis that has led to violence and displacement throughout my country. I admit that I am still wary, but I have new hope for the future of my country."

Throughout the week, the group continued to work and pray together and talk about what brought them hope. Florian, who was from Munich, Germany, said that he was not a particularly religious person, yet the week spent meditating and looking for things that give him hope had started to change how he saw the world around him. He shared with the group his worry that he would lose this new insight when he returned home. Florian proposed that this group set up a blog to which group members would post an entry each week on what they saw that made them hopeful. They named the blog *tumaini*, which means "hope" in Swahili.

Over the next many months, the group continued to blog together. Rev. Samantha found it particularly helpful as she finished seminary and began to look for a call. Whenever she felt anxious or cynical, she would read her friends' entries about hopeful and promising things all over the world. She also shared insights from the blog with her nearby friends.

After about a year, some of the original members of the group began to taper off. Yet something surprising had happened. It turned out that Rev. Samantha had not been the only group member to share the blog entries. Every member had done so. In addition, people from around the world had discovered the *tumaini* blog on their own. Friends of friends of the original group had expanded out like a spiderweb.

Florian continued to maintain the site as new contributors came and went. Maintaining the site was a way he found to refocus his attention on the world around him; instead of looking for problems to be solved, he looked for new life that needed to be nurtured.

Even after other members of the group began to taper off, Rev. Samantha and Rev. Wangari continued to blog and e-mail each other. Shortly after Rev. Samantha received the call to First Church in Middletown, Rev. Wangari was called to be a pastor in Kisumu. Rev. Wangari was overflowing with hope as she began working with an overflowing school. She talked about how exciting it was that more families could afford to send their children to school. Rev. Samantha was overflowing with excitement, too, as the members of First Church Middletown found renewed energy to open up themselves to the growing downtown, where the church was located.

In an e-mail, Rev. Samantha asked Rev. Wangari, "How can we support one another in these new, exciting endeavors?"

The question, which was also posted on the *tumaini* blog site, created a stir. Readers shared a multitude of suggestions. Florian became excited about what could happen in these two ministries. The result was that Rev. Samantha brought a team from her church to Kisumu to help in the new school and teach classes. They led a worship service and participated in Bible studies in the city. It was an eye-opening adventure for members of First Church Middletown. The next summer, Rev. Wangari brought a group to Middletown. They worked in vacation Bible school and reached out to the Kenyan community nearby. The result was the reception of many of the Kenyans into the congregation.

Florian followed all this with much interest. Though he was still hesitant to join an established church, he found life in the spiritual adventure of his friends. The other bloggers, who were more spiritual than religious, also found their faith invigorated.

The result was that on one day of the year, World Communion Sunday, they all linked together in a sort of electronic Pentecost. The congregation at Middletown sat in their pews. The congregation in Kisumu gathered in the gym of the school. Florian and the others gathered in front of laptops in their kitchens or at the local coffee shop.

At the appropriate moment, Rev. Samantha and Rev. Wangari said together, "Eat this bread and drink from this cup." They all ate and drank as one.

The world became a little smaller, and the church became a whole lot larger.

Chapter 23

What's the Point?

KATHLEEN COOK OWENS

I have read a lot of material about young adults in the church, the need to reach out to young adults, how to reach out, panic attacks about the dearth of rising church leadership. While much of it makes valid points about technology, changing ways of viewing the world, and the need to revitalize the church, it never seems to get very far beyond the printed page or possibly the margins of the church. All too often, young adults are overlooked or pushed down on the priority list as something that would be nice to do if there was more money or time. There is a part of me that understands this mentality. I have been supported and funded to attend one conference after another for young adults, all aimed at inspiring us and sending us out to shake up the ministry for young adults in our local community. I meet amazing people, get all excited, and then come home and the excitement fizzles. It seems like nothing is coming out of the experience provided. I try to start something new, to draw my friends in, to tell them what exciting new things are happening in the church. Invariably, the reply comes back: "What's the point?"

To a generation that, for the most part, was raised with little or no contact with the church, the church seems irrelevant. There are many opportunities to explore one's spirituality, in yoga or meditation classes, book groups, and support groups. There are a wide array of virtual and actual communities for fellowship from Facebook, to fantasy football leagues, to the local coffee shop. There are various and sundry ways to engage in social witness and justice through community organizations, our schools or workplaces, and even the decisions we make as consumers. It can be hard to explain what is different about what the church has to offer.

Difficulties in speaking about the church arise because, for those raised without much direct connection to the church and even for those who were raised in the church, our image of the church is shaped not by the church but by the media. We see the judgment and the arguments. The church becomes the people protesting school curriculum, the reporting on ongoing battles over who can be and who cannot be ordained, the people on street corners asking if you have been saved, the televangelists, the leaders of megachurches, and political leaders pointing to Jesus for their inspiration. The images are jumbled and confusing, to say the least, and, for most people, entirely negative. When was the last time you heard a positive news story about a church? The predominant media image of the church in the United States may not be fair, but we still have to deal with it directly, especially when reaching out to young adults.

I believe that the Reformed tradition has a very important witness to offer to young adults. We declare that we are a church reformed and always reforming. We are about witnessing to the here and now. We do not always live into this, but we profess it nonetheless. We also emphasize God's grace over God's judgment. We need to find ways to share our understanding of God's grace, and the transformative power that it holds, with a new generation. But we also need to be ready for how that generation may transform us. How can we get past the image of an arguing and divided church and instead present a church filled with grace and understanding, ready to be reformed and renewed for the world today? If we can counteract the media image by presenting ourselves in a new way, people might begin to see the point.

There is an added complication. In order to witness to young adults, we need to be ready to participate in a crash course in Christian formation. It can no longer be assumed that people know even the basic Bible stories and pieces of church history. My college Bible courses were filled with English majors who were seeking a better understanding of the biblical references in literature. They had never heard the story of the exodus, or of Mary and Joseph finding no room at the inn. We cannot assume that young adults know about Noah's ark or the feeding of the five thousand, much less the Reformation or differences between denominations. There is a lot of wisdom in the conversations of previous generations on common baptism, recognition of our ministries, and other crucial statements about our unity as a whole church. However, to move forward in these conversations, we are going to have to take a few steps backward. To launch straight into our differences, even in celebrating our diversity, can add to the argumentative image of the church that is too often portrayed in the media. Going straight to conversations about the finer points of our unity will soar over the heads of newcomers. How can we work together to continue our conversations while also educating and bringing new voices and views on board?

Then there is the unavoidable topic in any conversation about reaching out to young adults: technology. How can we be intentional about incorporating technology into our ministry in helpful ways? It is not helpful to have a Facebook group for the sake of having a Facebook group. We need to be intentional about the goals and reasons behind the use of modern technology. An effective use of technology is crucial for reforming the church to meet the needs of today. How can we connect people, support, inspire, and educate them? We need to ask these questions first, and then consider how current technology can help. The purpose has to come first, not the new gadget.

There are young adults out there and searching. There are also barriers for the church to overcome, not the least of which is budget cuts, especially in the formation of young adults. The Reformed tradition has a unique and important witness for young adults seeking a relevant church where they will find the grace and love of God and the community of believers. There is a point for having church, but we have work to do. Reaching out to young adults, helping us to find a home, is a challenge for all levels of the church, and it is often most effective when done in conjunction with ecumenical partners. The two or three local churches who cooperate for a campus ministry, the three or four others who sponsor the book group at the coffee shop, regional bodies that work together on young adult conference and support its outcomes, and the leadership opportunities available at all levels. I have heard Rev. Clifton Kirkpatrick and countless other leaders in our churches speak about the importance of the opportunities provided for them as young adults. For our future, we as a whole church need to be intentional about the opportunities we provide for young adults to be transformed by the power of God's grace as we experience it in our community. The church also needs to be open to the transformation that we as young adults will bring.

Chapter 24

Ecumenical Formation from a Layperson's Perspective

The Prodigal Presbyterian

EDWARD CHAN

My former campus minister, who serves an ecumenical ministry at a large private university, was lamenting the difficulty in maintaining financial support from each of the four supporting denominations. This time it was the United Methodists. "The Methodists," she said, "are concerned that if their students are exposed to other denominations, they will end up leaving the Methodist Church when they graduate."

"But if that's the case," I replied, "there's also the possibility that students from other denominations will be attracted to the Methodist Church and go there when they graduate. And since the Methodist Church outnumbers the Presbyterian Church three to one, they should come out ahead in the long run. Look at me: these days I often worship at a Methodist congregation.

"But," I added, "don't tell the Presbyterians I told you that."

Alas, the secret is out. I am a member of the Presbyterian Church (U.S.A.) who is not currently worshiping at a Presbyterian church. This has surprised people who have known me to be an active Presbyterian over the years, and perhaps disappointed a few of them. I grew up in a Chinese Presbyterian congregation. In college I attended a campus ministry funded by the Presbyterian Church and pastored by a Presbyterian minister. Later I became active in the national church, serving the denomination's higher education and student ministry committees. While in graduate school I represented the PC(USA) as a delegate to the 23rd General Council of the World Alliance of Reformed Churches. I recently completed service as chair of the PC(USA) Committee on Ecumenical Relations.

And yet, as much as the Presbyterian Church has nurtured me through my life, the ecumenical movement has been right by its side. The campus ministry I attended is an ecumenical partnership of four denominations, who realized that together they could maintain a presence on campus—paying a minister and having a critical mass of active students—that they could not do on their own. My entry into the work of the national church came through the conferences of the Council for Ecumenical Student Christian Ministries (CESCM), the U.S. member movement of the World Student Christian Federation. My experience at WARC opened my eyes to the global church and let me see how we looked through their eyes. So for me, it has been literally true, that to be Presbyterian is to be ecumenical.

As ecumenical as I was, all my life I have been a member of congregations of the Presbyterian Church (U.S.A.). But one day I found myself depleted, looking at Sunday worship as a chore, wishing I could stay home with a good Christian book or magazine instead. I was in need of spiritual first aid. Having been ecumenically formed as part of my Presbyterian formation, I decided to take the opportunity to explore other churches. First it was a Methodist congregation, a familiar home away from home. Then a Catholic church with a distinctly modern mass, where praise music meets the Great Prayer of Thanksgiving. Then a progressive, politically active, yet High-Church Episcopal congregation, complete with smells and bells. It has been refreshing to be away from the Presbyterian Church.

Executives in my home denomination who are reading this essay and eyeing their membership figures are no doubt getting nervous right about now. Some might be lamenting my wandering as a failure of my church to cement in me a Presbyterian identity. Some may see this as evidence of the dangers of the ecumenical movement. For although the Presbyterian Church (U.S.A.) *Book of Order* says that "the Church is called to undertake [its] mission even at the risk of losing its life," I suspect that few ever thought that suffering for one's faith would include turning loyal members into Anglicans.

Denominational executives may have good reason to worry. I am not alone in my wandering. According to a 2008 survey from the Pew Forum on Religion & Public Life, in the United States, only 40 percent of those who grew up Presbyterian would still identify themselves as Presbyterian.[1] Younger people (which I define as those under forty, if for no other reason than to include myself in the category) are particularly mobile: of those under forty who have changed religious affiliations from their childhood, one-fourth stayed within their tradition, but three-fourths have changed to another religious tradition or to having no religious affiliation.[2]

My worry for the Presbyterian Church is not for the 30 percent of former Presbyterians who have left for other mainline denominations. It is not for the 27 percent who have left for churches in the evangelical tradition. It is not even for the 15 percent who have left for non-Protestant churches or for other religions. My worry is for the 24 percent of former Presbyterians who now say they have no religious affiliation. All churches—those that are shrinking as well as those that are growing—are simultaneously gaining and losing members. But the category that is gaining the most "members" is the unaffiliated category, with three times as many people entering as there are leaving.

In such a time as this, churches should spend less time and energy worrying about their own denomination, less time and energy competing with each other, and instead spend more time and energy uniting to combat the common enemy: the growth in the numbers of those unaffiliated with any religion. The early efforts in the modern ecumenical movement were marked by a desire to cooperate in overseas evangelism and mission, such as in the 1910 Edinburgh conference. Our understandings of evangelism and mission have evolved since then, and today the greatest mission field may well be our own backyard. Perhaps it is a time for churches to return to a vision of shared ministry, for the purposes of growing the church universal.

As its national budget declines, I have seen the Presbyterian Church (U.S.A.) cut its contributions to the programming of ecumenical councils, eliminate staffing and funding for ecumenical formation, and now eliminate staffing and funding for its college student ministries. The denomination has turned inward, focusing on building its own brand: its own new church development, its own relief work, its own overseas missionaries. These are good and valuable programs, and Presbyterians do have a right to be proud of their work. But these are also things that could just as well be done ecumenically.

What if, instead, we had an ecumenical vision of ministry? An ecumenical vision of mission? An ecumenical vision of church growth and evangelism? With such a vision, it would not be necessary for programs to be housed in our own denomination for us to consider it "ours." In areas where no one church can afford their own program, an ecumenical partnership could result in retaining at least one staff person, to be shared by all. Alternatively, in areas where each church does maintain its own program, the churches could direct their staffs to work in cooperation with the corresponding programs of the partner churches, resulting in one stronger program instead of several separate weaker ones. To avoid duplication of efforts, churches might even outsource certain programming efforts to each other: "We'll keep our environmental justice program and share our programming resources with you; you keep your hunger ministry program and share your programming with us." It should not matter whose brand it is. As a speaker at one conference asked, "What, after all, is the uniquely Presbyterian response to global warming?"

Lest you think that ecumenical cooperation is limited to programming work, consider this: what if, instead of trying to plant new churches on its own, the

Presbyterian Church (U.S.A.) were to engage in all new church development and evangelism efforts in conjunction with its full communion partners? In a country where brand loyalty to denominational labels is weak, even among our current members, would not a combined approach do more to reach the unchurched, who have no denominational affiliation to begin with?

We can do more together than we can do apart. A stronger combined ministry, with stronger local congregations, blessed with the gifts that different traditions bring, could do more to attract new members, and do more to keep existing members from falling into the ranks of the unaffiliated . . . as I could have, except for the ecumenical movement. The question is not whether combined ministries are feasible. The question is whether the leaders of my denomination and of our partner denominations would have the courage to go this route. Would we be prepared to risk our (denominational) lives in order to save them?

The jury is still out as to when I will return to the Presbyterian Church. My spiritual life is getting back on track. I attend worship regularly again. I am being spiritually nourished, in "Faith and Order" as well as "Work and Life." I seem to have found a new congregation to join. And yet I have not transferred my membership. I cannot bring myself to give up being Presbyterian. Far from ecumenical engagement diluting my Presbyterianism, worshiping in non-Presbyterian settings has heightened my sense of being Presbyterian, even as I have come to appreciate, and indeed have been rescued by, the gifts that other traditions have to offer.

But if I am a Presbyterian not attending a Presbyterian church, what kind of Presbyterian does that make me? A lapsed Presbyterian? A prodigal Presbyterian? An ecumenical Presbyterian? Whatever I am, it certainly beats being an unaffiliated Presbyterian.

Ad majorem Dei gloriam. To the greater glory of God.

Chapter 25

You, Me, and Us

Young Adults and the Future of Christian Diversity

AIMEE MOISO

One Wednesday afternoon, Megan[1] came to see me in my campus ministry office. Raised Lutheran (Evangelical Lutheran Church in America, ELCA), the sophomore at this Catholic university has found community and fellowship through an evangelical Christian campus club, whose praise services are attended weekly by both Catholics and Protestants (mainliners and evangelicals[2]) alike. But Megan had become uncomfortable with the club's language of "true" Christianity. A narrow doctrine espoused by some student leaders left little room for questions or uncertainty, and Megan wasn't sure how to voice her opinion in that climate. "I hate when we break into small groups," she said, "because I never know what to say. I don't feel like I can be honest with my beliefs or doubts. I'm always relieved when we're done with that part of the evening."

Some hours later I donned my liturgical robes and processed into an inaugural mass for the new university president. Two faculty from the religious studies department walked with me: another Presbyterian pastor, and a Catholic woman recently ordained as a Zen priest. We sat in the second row in our vestments, and the rest of the procession—about sixty Jesuit priests and the local Catholic bishop—took their places on the front altar. During the mass, the congregation was issued an open invitation to the Eucharist table, but wearing our decidedly un-Catholic liturgical garb, none of the three of us felt it appropriate to receive.[3] Afterward the bishop greeted us warmly. A Presbyterian faculty member gushed about how included she felt in having us there. But one of the other Catholic campus ministers commented to me later how ridiculous it seemed to him to have Protestant clergy process and then not participate in Eucharist when, as he put it, "you are so clearly part of the family."

The next morning I met with Mike, a student who is part of a church with Southern Baptist affiliations. In our conversation, I asked him about his connection to that denomination. "We affirm the Southern Baptist statement of faith," he said nonchalantly, "but denominations aren't really that important anymore. These days, it's much more about networking."

In my short time as a Presbyterian clergywoman serving as a campus minister at a Catholic Jesuit university in California, my work has brought into clear focus the current dichotomy of American ecumenism: how far we have come, and how far we have to go.

At first glance, the Catholic/Protestant divide seems the most pronounced. Not long ago, I received an e-mail from a student asking for my help with a project on the role of women in the church. But she proposed her topic like this: "I hope to explore some of the differences between women in the two dominant religions in the United States, Christianity and Catholicism." I often hear this distinction between "Christians" and "Catholics." Most Catholic students describe themselves as "Catholic" rather than Christian, and some I've talked to are reluctant to consider themselves the same religion as Protestants, especially conservative or fundamentalist evangelicals. "We all follow Christ," said one, expressing a common sentiment, "but we're just so *different* in how we understand that."

Divergent understandings of how to follow Christ surely are at the heart of the historic divisions of the church. A triumph of the U.S. ecumenical movement of the twentieth century has seen relative fluidity between and among various Protestant denominations today. Conciliar ecumenism has helped to dispel much of the animosity that once existed between Lutherans and Baptists or Methodists and Presbyterians, and a recent Pew Forum study indicates that more than one in three adult Protestants in the United States have switched denominational affiliation within the Protestant tradition in their adulthood.[4] The majority of Protestant students I encounter reflect this cultural shift. Those who were raised Protestant—mainline, evangelical, nondenominational—typically describe themselves as "Christian" when asked about their religion. Little consideration is given to denominational affiliation; what is important to them is a common desire to seek and follow Christ. Most students are unaware, however, that the freedom and flexibility they now enjoy reflects the ecumenical efforts of previous generations.

Unfortunately, the nonspecific Christianity that seems to be the norm among Protestant university students can be a double-edged sword. The breakdown of denominational specificity and lack of consistent, strong Christian education as mainline churches have declined has meant that even those who grew up in the church, especially mainliners, are often at a loss to know how to dig deeply into their own roots or claim their own heritage. A sophomore raised Methodist said to me that while she really loved the church of her youth, she is "not really sure what it means to be Methodist anyway." She "learned about Noah and Moses in Sunday school" but did not acquire tools to articulate her own beliefs today.

Simultaneously, the more conservative or fundamentalist Protestant students, despite being relatively unconcerned about denominational affiliation, tend to want to draw doctrinal lines around who is in and who is out; they often see themselves as true believers among false or misguided Others. For many of them, the entire conceptualization of faith is predicated on being right, even at the risk of being alone or divided from others. Students who are part of these communities also firmly believe that their understanding of Christianity is complete, pure, and undefiled by context or culture.[5]

Meanwhile, other Christian students, both Protestant and Catholic, find themselves deeply uncomfortable with conservative fundamentalism. Raised in an era of unprecedented globalization and pluralism, they wrestle with embarrassment over Christianity's sordid past of colonization and Western domination; they find themselves at odds with Christian claims about ultimate truth, infallibility, morality, and "one way to salvation." While they love the church and the Christian faith, they have been given few resources to reconcile traditional church teaching with their encounters of religious and cultural diversity. In this milieu, college kids are often left feeling conflicted about the nature and purpose of faith, disconnected and alienated from the institutional church, and searching for something that will attend to both the richness of Christian history and authentic, relevant, personal experience today.

Since I have been trained in ecumenical studies and serve as "the Protestant among the Catholics," I frequently referred to the idea of "Christian unity" the first year I worked at the university. I made a poster defining ecumenism and posted it on my office door. I created a student "Intern for Christian Unity" position. I preached at the student mass and held other events during the Week of Prayer for Christian Unity. I talked about the need to come together across our differences, recognize our common baptism, and affirm all we share.

My efforts gained little traction. The abstract concept of "Christian unity" does not have much meaning for students raised without knowledge of historic Christian divisions. Many students grew up in households with parents from two different traditions. The well-attended campus masses offer an open invitation to the Table, wherein the choice to receive is up to the individual, and in general Catholic students seem undaunted when Protestant friends join them for Eucharist. Catholic students, staff, and even priests freely receive communion from me when they attend Protestant worship. For most students, the lack of obvious conflict among denominations—or in their eyes, even real difference among them—signifies that the historical divisions of the church seem irrelevant or passé, if they are aware of such divisions at all. The only students I know who refrain from receiving Eucharist at Catholic mass because of historical Christian divisions are Orthodox, and many still attend and enjoy the masses regularly anyway.

The few students who have resisted the idea of Christian unity do so because they fear it will lead to a kind of generic melting pot of Christianity, in which specificity is lost. For conservative or fundamentalist students, the concern is over watering down what they see as essentials in Christian doctrine. Roman Catholic students who love the ritual of the Catholic Mass fear losing the tradition and sacramental practice of liturgy, both of which lie at the heart of their faith.

In response to these experiences, some months ago I subtly changed tack—and language. I altered the job description of the Intern for Christian Unity, calling it the "Intern for Christian Diversity" and emphasizing how the position will work to honor and explore various expressions of Christianity on campus. The results were immediate. The candidates I interviewed for the new internship quickly identified with the concept of the position and spoke articulately about why Christian diversity is needed on our campus. They easily expressed ways in which partnership across different traditions might be possible and important, and how we might learn from each other. As I floated the language around other areas of my work—with other Campus Ministry interns and staff, mainline students, the Orthodox Christian Fellowship group—I found similar reactions. The language of Christian diversity seemed almost instantly to open a different kind of conversation, in which each is free to explore and deepen one's own Christian faith while being connected to others who might understand or celebrate Christianity differently.

In his book *Christian Unity and Christian Diversity,* John Macquarrie wrote in 1974:

> Diversity is just as essential as unity to the well-being of the Christian church. To combine unity with freedom is a very difficult task, and the temptations to uniformity are very great. But a truly Christian unity can never be a tightly knit affair. It must leave room not just for the preservation but [also] for the continuing development of the rich heritage of different Christian traditions in which men and women of very different types have come to know the inexhaustible resources of the Christian faith.[6]

Thirty-five years later, Macquarrie's claim is more relevant than ever. While U.S. and international ecumenical movements have used language of unity-in-diversity and diversity-in-unity in various ways over the past decades, a reimagined and reasserted vision of Christian diversity is critical to ecumenism once again, both for young adults who are looking for direction in a complicated and pluralistic world, and for the health and well-being of denominations struggling for survival. It is not simply a matter of reinserting "diversity" language into the ecumenical movement, but that the ecumenical movement—and indeed the church and churches themselves—must recognize again and anew that finding and honoring our diversity are actually the only way we will come to unity together. Says Macquarrie, "We must be as much in earnest with pluralism as we are with unity, recognizing that both have their justification in Christian theology" (18). If the university were to embrace this perspective, I imagine exciting results would follow:

1. For Roman Catholic students, the idea of "Christian diversity" offers a way to engage the language of "Christian" and to explore the broader Christian tradition—and themselves as part of it. It helps to dispel fear of losing or diluting Catholic identity, because particular practice is honored and appreciated; but it also suggests that others, too, are sincere in their faith in Jesus Christ. For those who are unfamiliar with Protestant traditions and perhaps see non-Catholic Christians as another religion entirely, just saying "Christian diversity" opens a new perspective in which Christian faith might be something shared across traditional boundaries.

2. For Protestant students of mainline traditions, "Christian diversity" allows for specificity at a time of denominational identity crises: in the context of Christian diversity, it is okay to self-identify as a Methodist Christian, or a Presbyterian Christian, or a Lutheran Christian. But more important, it encourages knowledge and understanding of what traditions mean and are, and from what roots they have come. In mainline denominations struggling for survival and split internally along political and social lines, thinking in terms of "Christian diversity" gives permission to name what is unique to a tradition and what is shared with others, and thus how we might understand and claim our identity more fully while also building new partnerships and repairing old breaches.

3. For Eastern and Oriental Orthodox students, "Christian diversity" signifies that, though they are a small minority on campus, they are remembered and included as part of the Christian family. This is especially important for Orthodox students, who feel distanced from the dominant culture of the university by being both religiously *and* culturally or ethnically distinct. Linking

the word "Christian" with "diversity" suggests that differences are respected, even as we are part of one Christian family tree. Since many Orthodox students understand their traditions to be among the most ancient in Christianity, a focus on Christian diversity encourages them to claim their heritage while seeing it as a point of commonality with later Christian expressions.

4. For conservative and fundamentalist students, "Christian diversity" serves as a reminder that no one tradition has a complete view or understanding of God, Jesus, or Christianity. Such language challenges competitive and triumphal understandings of "one true church" or "true Christianity." It also connotes engagement and participation with others who might see things differently but who also seek to follow Jesus Christ. It remains to be seen whether the most fundamentalist students will be willing to agree that diversity in Christianity should be valued; yet for many, a slight broadening of perspective would come as welcome relief from having to always discern and then follow what is "right."

An obvious final question is this: What kind of diversity are we talking about? Denominational? Theological? Doctrinal? Liturgical? Perhaps defining diversity will be as slippery and difficult as the still unanswered ecumenical question: What kind of unity are we talking about? But for twenty-first-century ecumenism, and young adults in particular, the question "How are we the same?" does not prompt nearly as rich a conversation as "How could engaging our differences enrich us and help us to know God and ourselves better?"

For all of us, "Christian diversity" calls to our attention the myriad ways in which the Christian tradition has changed over history and continues to respond to and be transformed by God in the contexts in which we live today. Our denominational particularities should not be overlooked, but they are also not the only way or even the primary ways in which we are diverse or divided. As we continue to seek God's leading and reconciliation, "Christian diversity" implies we need one another, and we need to bring our complex identities to the conversation. We do not have to give up our heritage in order to be the body of Christ, and neither are we complete without each other.

Chapter 26

Whenever You Eat This Bread and Drink This Cup

Being a Communion of Churches

NEAL D. PRESA

The cup of blessing that we bless, is it not a sharing in the blood of Christ? The bread that we break, is it not a sharing in the body of Christ? Because there is one bread, we who are many are one body, for we all partake of the one bread.

1 Corinthians 10:16–17

*L*et me share with you two stories from the Caribbean. The Executive Committee of the World Alliance of Reformed Churches met in 2007 at Tunapuna, Trinidad, where it took formal action to adopt the name "World Communion of Reformed Churches" instead of the proposed name, "World Reformed Communion." Intense discussion and debate ensued as to what exactly was meant by the term "communion." Unlike episcopally ordered churches that understand their intrachurch relationships as "communion" (e.g., the Roman Catholic Church, the Anglican Communion), the Reformed tradition has steered clear of speaking of our ecclesiastical polity as a communion. We are comfortable with "fellowship" terminology, or even "alliance," but "communion" evoked concerned reactions. Underlying those concerns were fears that confessional subscriptionism, hierarchical structuring of the new organization, and mandates for funding commitments would result. We in the Reformed tradition have historically prided ourselves on doing things "decently and in order" (1 Cor. 14:40), but with a careful caveat that such ordering should not impose on our individual consciences of what we have discerned and determined the Lord to be saying to us as individuals or to our own churches. What, then, does it mean to be a communion of Reformed churches? What will it require to fully live into the reality of being a communion?

137

The second story comes from Guyana. At the 2008 joint assembly of the Caribbean and North America Area Council of WARC (CANAAC) and the Caribbean and North America Council for Mission (CANACOM) in Georgetown, Guyana, delegates visited the Sophia Presbyterian Church in a rural, impoverished section outside of Georgetown. Farm animals freely roam the unpaved, muddy road alongside barefoot children. The gathering space for the Sophia church is a small concrete structure, with openings for an entrance door and windows along the side aisle, but with no actual window or door. On entering this space, we see movable wooden bench pews arranged in theater style, facing the chancel area, which holds a pulpit with a wooden cross affixed to it. About 120 worshipers congregate in that space; they are served by Pastor Prasaud, called to minister there without any financial support from the Guyana Presbyterian Church because of the presbytery's lack of funds. Church members who greet us tell us of many children who look forward to attending Bible classes there, a church family that is excited to worship and fellowship together, and Pastor Prasaud, with his contagious smile exuding strength and joy in this place. Seeing no baptismal font and no communion table, I inquire whether the church baptizes and communes, and if so, how?

The response: they baptize people in the lake and river. As for the Lord's Table, they have not been able to do that because they do not have the financial means to obtain even a chalice and paten.

After returning to the United States, I wondered to some colleagues what it would mean for us to reconsider the Reformation "marks" of the church: preaching of the sacraments, faithful administration of the sacraments, and—in the case of the Scots Confession, Bucer, and Bullinger—church discipline. Would the Sophia Presbyterian Church fit the definition of "church" if it did not celebrate the Eucharist as formally understood,[1] but practiced table fellowship among its members and within the rural community in which they lived and belonged? How can practices shape our understanding of what communion is, and vice versa?

If the fears and concerns of the Trinidad meeting come to fruition and we become a communion of churches that discipline one another for not purely subscribing to Reformed tenets, then churches like Sophia Presbyterian Church and a whole host of churches in the United States and around the world that are embodying the gospel in different ways will be questioned about their integrity and credibility.

Instead, we need to call for what the late Yale theologian Hans Frei coined "generous orthodoxy," in which he explained, "Generosity without orthodoxy is nothing, but orthodoxy without generosity is worse than nothing."[2]

As we move forward as the World Communion of Reformed Churches, what we need is a robust sense of our communion identity that has the following key characteristics:

- Grounded in the Trinity
- A closer connection of global-regional-local praxis
- Worship as the essence of the church's identity

A fuller treatment of these three key points is necessary, but for our purposes I will sketch contours of what a communion-ecclesiological identity might look like as the WCRC moves forward.

Grounded in the Trinity

The communion that we seek to inhabit within the WCRC, like the visible unity for which the ecumenical movement has labored over many decades, is a gift and work of the triune God.[3] The perfect, loving, mutual communion of the Father, the Son, and the Holy Spirit is extended to the world by Christ in the Holy Spirit; the purpose of this extension is to embrace us in the divine fellowship and call us to give ethical and visible expression of that communion with one another.

The proposed constitution and Articles of Union of the WCRC put forward by the joint WARC-REC executive committees lift up this central conviction that the triune God constitutes the communion, desires the communion, and enables the communion to be lived out in spite of the intrachurch and interchurch disagreements that still exist among us.

In his reflections after completing a term as deputy general secretary of the WCC, and before his election as general secretary of the WCC, Konrad Raiser lifted up two key themes of a future ecumenical paradigm: "the *'oikos'* structure of the *oikumenē* and a social understanding of the Trinity."[4] He explained the relatedness of *oikos* and the Trinity this way: "The 'household' as an open space for living and the communion of the Trinity as the reciprocal relatedness of those who remain distinct and different are symbols, holding two opposite poles together in tension."[5]

Similar to Joseph Small's seven listings of implications for a communion ecclesiology (see note 3 for this chapter), Raiser discusses the "house rules" of the *oikumenē* within the common *oikos* we all live in: "dialogue and striving for truth,"[6] "sharing in solidarity" (which includes the sharing of resources and power),[7] mutual learning,[8] and hospitality.[9]

In lifting up the *oikos* metaphor for the ecumenical movement, Raiser understands communion to be about living into the "one household of life" in which the triune God calls us to participate and which God actually enjoins us to realize and discern. He speaks of the delicate ecology that characterizes this Trinity-centered, Trinity-formed household as one that lives constantly in the tension of "boundary and openness, independence and relationship, rest and movement, the familiar and the alien, continuity and discontinuity."[10]

Being grounded in the Trinity will mean the following for the World Communion of Reformed Churches and its member churches:

- Renegotiating uses and understanding of one's position of power and resources vis-à-vis the other member churches and the WCRC as a whole
- Mutual confession and healing of the times and places in which we have been complicit in lording over Others with our power and resources
- Broadening and deepening our relationships with traditions that have not been at the Table, especially non-Reformed Christians and people of other faith traditions

Raiser concludes his reflections by citing former WCC general secretary Philip Potter, in Potter's report to the WCC Vancouver Assembly, wherein he emphasized our common calling to be the household of the triune God, a calling that demands "confessing, learning, participating, sharing, healing, reconciliation, unity and expectancy, to the glory of God, Father, Son, and Holy Spirit."[11]

A Closer Connection of Global-Regional-Local Praxis

Related to the communion orientation of the Trinity is the notion of the mutual interdependence of all to the one, and the one to the all. Thus, when we speak of the communion of Reformed churches, we cannot confine our discussions and actions to the work of the Geneva secretariat of the WCRC, or to the various area councils, or to the head offices of our various member churches. To hold the Trinity as the focal and pivot point of the witness of the WCRC is to necessarily consider and account for the common, mutual, interconnected work of the whole with the sum of the parts and with each individual part.

With diminished financial and staff resources, the WCRC will need to find creative and new ways in doing its work. Member churches need to see the tangible relevance of why the future viability of the communion is important to the Reformed witness and to their own witness in their geographical contexts. Because the Geneva secretariat cannot be expected to be all things to all churches all the time, the notion of being a global communion of churches means that though programs and core priorities are determined at the global and conciliar levels, the consultations, implementations, and interpretations occur most pointedly at the regional and local levels.[12]

The WCRC, like the ecumenical movement generally, can ill afford speaking and acting in the abstract. One staff member of the WCC told a recent regional consultation of Covenanting for Justice that when World Bank and IMF officials gave the WCC the opportunity to offer an alternative solution to global economic recession, the WCC representatives asked the officials if they had heard of the Accra Confession and the Covenanting for Justice process. The response? The World Bank and the IMF had never ever heard of those proposals! Nearly two decades of work led to the eventual adoption of the Accra Confession in 2004, and yet it remains unseen and unknown in the corridors and conference tables of global monetary institutions.

Let me be clear. This is not to diminish the importance of the Accra Confession, the Covenanting for Justice process, or any other confession or conciliar statement or program. All are important, and it is essential that the church speak prophetically when the signs of the times require such a word. But the church must speak wisely, bringing the witness of the triune God to the right places, at the right time, with strategies that engage not only church actors but also all sectors of society. We cannot just speak to ourselves within the church about global issues; the WCRC needs to have a vital witness in the world, engaging partners, religious and secular, to address the economic, ecological, moral, and spiritual ills of our time.

The mutual interdependency of global-regional-local actors, grounded in and propelled by the Trinity, ensures that there is accountability and sharing of resources from top to bottom and bottom to top. Analogically speaking, the persons of the triune Godhead did not confine their divine love to one another, but willingly set out to create and then embrace the created order in their divine communion. So too, the WCRC and its member churches, by the communion's very nature, are mutually interdependent in planning, programming, and implementing. After all, our confession as Christians has always been that "Jesus is Lord," a total lordship over heaven and earth and everything in it. Such lordship needs to be brought to bear upon the decision making of all sectors of society. A mutual interdependency of global-regional-local actors across the board will enable a broad and deep witness of the lordship of the triune God.

Worship as the Very Essence of the Church's Identity

It is easy to compartmentalize the church's worship, the church's mission, and the church's justice work. We form committees that specialize in these areas, and we congratulate ourselves at the organized pace at which the church, like a well-oiled machine, is operating. Some will argue that the dichotomy of mission and justice is false because we cannot have one without the other; both are synonymous one to another. The church's mission is to do justice; doing justice is mission work. Others will argue that the church's identity is mission, to be a witness, to be sent to the world.

A communion that is grounded, constituted, shaped, and informed by the Trinity is a worshiping community at its core and at its periphery; worship is the very being of the church.[13] This means that all the church is and does is worship, or in the words of Hebrews, it is the church's "sacrifice of praise."[14] This is in keeping with the etymological significance of the term *leitourgia*, from which comes the word "liturgy." *Leitourgia* is a work done for the public good, that expresses one's commitment or pledge to the public; by doing it, the doers become more aware of their mutual responsibility for the common good and concretize their realization of their membership in the public.

The church cannot be seen merely as a community that equips in order to send. That is a large part of what the church is and does, but that is not its essence and that is not the point of its calling. The communion ecclesiology grounded, shaped, informed, and propelled by the Trinity is one that is *for* the Trinity, in which what the church is and does is directed toward gathering all of creation to the glory and praise of the triune God. To be sent as witnesses to the world is not an end or a means but is an act of worship. Worship is what defines the church as the church.

To be a communion of churches, therefore, is to find our raison d'être in worship, specifically in the celebration of the divine liturgy, the Eucharist. The WCRC will advance toward ecumenical convergence in the areas of Eucharist and ministry vis-à-vis the Roman Catholic Church, the Orthodox, and the Anglican Church when we see the centrality of the Eucharist in the life, work, and witness of the church, no less than in the very identity of the church.

It is at the Eucharist, connected to the proclamation of the gospel in sermon and Scripture, that the church hears/sees for the first time and is re-membered again and again as the people of God, the body of Christ, and the temple of the Spirit.[15] When the church is sent out to be God's witnesses, the missional church does not end its worship; the *leitourgia* continues as the church worships through service, doing justice, loving-kindness, equipping and discipling others. At dining tables, meeting tables, homeless soup-kitchen tables, the eucharistic Table is connected to all those; it provides the liturgical and upward definition to what happens at those Tables as the church bears witness to the triune God.

The World Communion of Reformed Churches will be more adept at living into the communion when we find our life, foundation, and purpose in the Trinity; when we see the mutual interdependence of the global-regional-local contexts and praxis; and when we come to the eucharistic Table soberly, humbly, expectantly, calling others to encounter the triune God in the breaking of bread and the drinking of the cup.

A New Bond in a Higher Calling

Clifton Kirkpatrick and Christian Unity

SAMUEL KOBIA

*I*n 2008 the General Assembly of the Presbyterian Church (U.S.A.) adopted a reaffirmation of that church's commitment to the ecumenical movement. This was the final assembly where Clifton Kirkpatrick served as stated clerk before his retirement from that office. The reaffirmation was one product of a consultation on Christian unity that Cliff had been instrumental in organizing. This consultation, held at Louisville, Kentucky, in September 2007, was the first major conference on the PC(USA)'s ecumenical stance since the 1983 Reunion of the northern and southern branches of that church.

One of the final sections of the General Assembly's ecumenical affirmation describes the connection between local and global expressions of Christianity: "The tasks of Christian witness, service, justice, and peacemaking are addressed by councils, alliances, and national churches, but also in local encounters, congregational interaction, and common prayer across traditional religious boundaries."[1]

One of the great contributions that Cliff Kirkpatrick has made to the church ecumenical arises from the continuing reminder he offers that Christian witness in the world is a seamless garment, a continuum running from personal faith and family interaction, through congregational and local experience, to the wider vistas of national, regional, confessional, and worldwide testimony to Christian unity. It is significant that his career has taken him from student work in Presbyterian parishes to urban interchurch ministries in the Texas cities of Dallas, Houston, and Fort Worth. After helping to coordinate interdenominational mission at the metropolitan level, he joined the national staff of the Atlanta-based Presbyterian Church in the U.S. as director of global mission. Largely on the basis of his experience in mission, evangelism, diaconal work, and advocacy, Cliff was eventually elected stated clerk of the General Assembly of the reunited PC(USA) and soon found himself in leadership positions of such organizations as the National Association of Ecumenical Staff, the National Council of Churches, Churches Uniting in Christ, and the World Alliance of Reformed Churches (WARC).

While serving on both the central and executive committees of the World Council of Churches, from December 1998 to February 2006, our friend Dr. Kirkpatrick frequently traced the connections between the different components of the ecumenical movement. He also recognized that the common search for unity has increasingly become a "countercultural calling" in a world of ethnic, confessional, and ideological isolation.[2] Even after he had been elected president of WARC, Cliff insisted that "Christian world communions do not exist for themselves but to strengthen the whole ecumenical movement." He also reminded us that, in the current upheavals of councils encouraging dialogue and cooperation, "we are witnessing changing patterns of church life worldwide. The present ecumenical structures are based on denominational structures that are disappearing. The problem is how to engage with new patterns of church life and at the same time stand against them when they take up stances that are against the gospel, such as attacking Islam or denying the equality of women."[3]

At the September 2007 consultation on the ecumenical stance of the Presbyterian Church (U.S.A.), Cliff Kirkpatrick accepted an invitation to present his list of the "top ten challenges facing twenty-first-century ecumenism." It is a snapshot of a key ecumenical leader's thinking at a crucial moment in the life of this movement; it demonstrates how Cliff's vision embraces the whole scope of Christian living, from the personal and local to the international and truly catholic. Here is a passage from one account of the consultation:

> Kirkpatrick expressed appreciation for the presence of participants from other denominations and ecumenical agencies because "we can't be ecumenical all by ourselves." Kirkpatrick offered what he considers to be the top ten challenges for twenty-first-century ecumenism:
>
> 1. Avoid reversing the Lund Principle [an ecumenical principle affirming that Christian churches should act together in all things except where, because of conscience, they are compelled to act separately from each other].
> 2. Renew the ecumenical vision for a postmodern church and world.
> 3. Reconcile with people of other faiths.
> 4. Broaden ecumenical conversations to include those who have shied away from traditional ecumenical groupings.
> 5. Ecumenical formation for a new generation.
> 6. Claim the ecumenical ethic of justice in the economy and the earth.

7. Renewal through an ecumenical spirituality.
8. Use the 500th anniversary of the Reformation [2017] as a time of ecumenical healing.
9. Next steps in Presbyterian/Reformed union and communion.
10. Meeting the ecumenical challenge within the PC(USA).[4]

Cliff Kirkpatrick is a consummately practical leader, always looking for concrete proposals to implement big ideas. Few people are better at guiding a group past obstacles to the solution of a problem. It is interesting that his outline list of ten contemporary challenges to the ecumenical movement does not provide how-to answers; it is more a list of conversation starters, an invitation to join in the early stages of a multilateral discussion. One of Cliff's great gifts is the ability to initiate and encourage dialogues aimed at forging instruments that are the creation of all and the property of all.

From his experience of exploring consensus-based decision making in WARC, culminating in the Accra conference of 2004, Cliff was able to provide direction for the WCC as it sought a means of moving beyond the tradition of parliamentary decision making in its governing bodies. Daring to venture into unfamiliar constitutional procedures was essential, he told us, because the ecumenical movement will prosper only if we achieve "common ownership of the decisions" reached by world communions and councils of churches.[5] In the same spirit, he supported early meetings of the Global Christian Forum and Christian Churches Together in the United States as they drew an unprecedented range of Christian bodies into conversation. This attitude of respect for the convictions of every party to a conversation is one of Cliff's defining characteristics and a primary source of his effectiveness as a minister of reconciliation.

I am profoundly grateful to Cliff for his continual emphasis on what is truly important in our quest for common ground: not the manufacture of strategies or structures, but the love we share and our proclamation of the gospel of Jesus Christ. This is how he and a colleague put it in addressing members of the Presbyterian Church (U.S.A.):

We hope that every congregation and every governing body will make a fresh commitment to sharing the gospel in word and deed in their own community and throughout the world. As we join together as a missionary people, determined to make a difference for the gospel in the world, we are confident that we will gain a new respect and love for one another.

It has been done before! It is hard to imagine any group more diverse than the group assembled in Jerusalem on that first Pentecost. They came from literally every continent, every race, and every social condition known in the Mediterranean world. Yet when they received the Holy Spirit, they set out with a passion for mission. As the book of Acts makes clear, their differences did not disappear, but they found a new bond in a higher calling.[6]

The twenty-first century's experimentation with new models of unity and cooperation has begun. Some endeavors show promise; others are already being rethought and overhauled. The essential thing, as Cliff Kirkpatrick keeps reminding us, is the spirit in which we take up our cause. By whatever means, we are still called together in faith "to maintain the unity of the Spirit in the bond of peace" (Eph. 4:3).

Epilogue

A Future for the Reformed Movement Worldwide?

CLIFTON KIRKPATRICK

All over the world we have recently completed a wonderful celebration of John Calvin's 500th birthday. We have also celebrated the witness of the Reformed churches, to which his movement gave birth half a millennium ago. God has done incredible things through this movement, and many of them have been celebrated in major events in places as diverse as Geneva, Paris, Seoul, Accra, Stellenbosch, São Paulo, and Montreat, North Carolina. In all of these locales—and many more—the focus has been not so much to glorify Calvin as to celebrate and reclaim his legacy, which has shaped our movement for these last five centuries.

During these celebrations we have focused on how Calvin's vision revolutionized Geneva by welcoming refugees, building a church centered on Word and sacrament, shaping a church order of shared leadership, reminding all of the sovereignty of God over all of life, and opening the Bible and its witness to Christ as the Word of God to all the people. It was a heady time in Geneva in the sixteenth century, but the revolution that Calvin led there did not stop at the walls of the old city of Geneva.

Throughout the sixteenth century and into the seventeenth, this Reformed vision spread out across Europe. Using the Academy, Calvin's great educational innovation, and based on Calvin's *summa theologica, The Institutes of the Christian Religion*, leaders were trained who took the Reformed movement and the Reformed vision of the church to Scotland, the Netherlands, Hungary, and many other parts of Europe. In the eighteenth century, that movement spread to North America, and in the nineteenth the seeds of the Reformed tradition began to be planted all around the world through the modern missionary movement. These seeds of the Reformed tradition, enriched by cultures all around the world, gave birth to a global Reformed movement.

149

However, when the World Alliance of Reformed Churches was born in 1875, it was exclusively a European and North American family, based on the demographics of the Reformed churches at that time, yet even more on the cultural blindness of our forebears, who failed to appreciate the dynamism of the Reformed movement in the global South. Even when construction was begun on the Reformation Wall to honor Calvin's 400th birthday, it was simply assumed that any depiction of the global spread of this Reformation movement would focus on leaders from Europe—with one representative from North America!

As we have now come to Calvin's 500th birthday, we are well aware that this Reformation is truly a global phenomenon, whose center and heart are now in the global South, where two-thirds of the world's 80 million Reformed Christians now reside. Though there are huge differences based on culture, resources, and political context, the Reformation movement that Calvin started in Geneva has made a major impact on all parts of the world and created a church community that has been a vehicle through which the gospel has been shared and God's justice upheld in vastly different corners of our globe over these 500 years. There is much to celebrate, and we have done that this past year!

But what of the future of our movement? Is the Calvin Jubilee the final or penultimate chapter for a Reformed tradition that has enriched the world for the last half a millennium but whose best days are behind it? In many parts of the world, that is a real and deeply held question. Or are these 500 years merely a prelude that has allowed the Reformed movement to be planted all around the world for the "mighty acts of God" that will be lived out through witness of Reformed Christians in the twenty-first century and for centuries to come after that? Is there a dynamic and redemptive future for the Reformed tradition?

That question is at the heart of this book. Over the last six years, it has been my unique privilege to serve as president of the World Alliance of Reformed Churches and, among other things, to visit at some depth with Reformed Christians in all parts of the globe. It has been a wonderful experience and, often at the same time, one that has led me to be deeply troubled about the prospects for the Reformed tradition and its witness as we move into the twenty-first century. I have come away from that with evidence that might lead one to believe that the best days of the Reformed tradition are behind us and with evidence to fill me with excitement that our best days lie ahead.

I want to use this essay to look at both sides of this question—to look deeply at the troubling signs that might make us doubt the vitality of the

Reformed tradition and at the signs of strength that should fill us with hope and lead us into the future with confidence. Hopefully, at the end of this exploration we will be clearer about the things from which God is calling us to repent and change and about the foundations of strength on which we might build our witness in the twenty-first century and beyond. I am convinced that God has a future, an exciting future, for Reformed Christians, but only if we face squarely our signs of weakness and build on our strengths.

Reasons to Doubt the Future of the Reformed Tradition

A Radically New World

The writer of the book of Revelation expressed his hopeful vision in the words, "Behold, I make all things new" (21:5 KJV). In imagining a totally new world, I wonder if he had any idea how dramatically things could change in the twenty-first century. It took 1,500 years from the beginning of the Common Era to double the sum of human knowledge, but now we double the sum of human knowledge every year. It is a time of incredibly fast change, where yesterday's verities no longer apply a year later. Ours is a movement deeply rooted in tradition, and yet we are in a time of incredibly fast-paced change, where adherence to tradition is not highly valued and where organizations that do place a high value on tradition often get left behind in the global marketplace of ideas.

Although Calvin brought radical change to Geneva, he was careful to build on the foundations of the apostolic faith, the church fathers, and the clear tradition of Scripture. He sought a well-ordered and disciplined world and did not seek to fundamentally overthrow the civil magistrates. The era in which we live—the era of economic globalization, instant communication, radical individualism, and a growing divide between the rich and the poor—would be exceptionally strange to Calvin, and it is often exceptionally strange to his heirs: us!

Change is all around us, especially in the church. A Christian world that we assumed to be Catholic, mainline Protestant, and Orthodox has been overturned in a few short years so that now the Pentecostal and charismatic churches form the second largest Christian group worldwide (after the Catholics). Patterns of worship and music are totally different than a generation ago. New technologies are changing how we worship, communicate with one another, and organize church life. Independent megachurches with no organic connection to any part of the wider Christian community are now flourishing in every part of the world. And the patterns of instant communication give us no excuse to ignore the vast injustices of our age.

Presbyterian and Reformed churches, faced with this incredible pace of change, often respond to all of this change by the standard rejoinder: "We've always done it this way." Calvin was a master at connecting the gospel message to emerging technologies, such as the printing press in his time, and we need to do the same. Many of the churches in the global South have made great strides in expressing Reformed life and worship in the cultural forms of their context, but far too many of us are still having difficulty relating to the new (and multiple) cultural forms in which our people worship God.

What has concerned me most as I have visited Reformed churches in almost every part of the world is that, almost without exception, the average age of participants in Reformed church congregations is older than the average age of that culture—and of many in the Pentecostal and evangelical megachurches. With the power and the challenge of the gospel, we must find fresh ways to reach out to new generations, and if we are to do that well, we must learn to communicate, worship, social network, and deal with the worldview emerging in our time.

Loss of Membership and Vitality

Although there are no universally verified global statistics, based on country-by-country statistics and observation, it is clear that Reformed churches are at best holding static and at worst declining in numbers. In the global North, most of our churches are clearly losing members. In my own church our membership is half of what we had in 1960, a pattern not limited to the Presbyterian Church (U.S.A.) but widely shared by churches in North America, Europe, Australia, and Japan.

While many of our churches are still growing in the global South, their growth is clearly being eclipsed by Pentecostal, prosperity gospel, and independent megachurches. Even our churches known for evangelism, spiritual vitality, and church growth, in places like Korea, have reached a plateau, and the years of rapid church growth seem to have passed. In other cases that we should never forget, our churches are not growing because they are facing active persecution or various forms of discrimination or because they are in cultures where Christians are fleeing. All of this makes it hard to grow the church and maintain a vital witness. One of the main reasons that we have global bodies like WARC and REC is to stand in solidarity with our churches in these situations.

Even more important than numbers is the lack of energy and spiritual vitality in too many of our churches. A few years ago, I had the privilege of visiting with our Reformed member churches in Germany. While there, I had the opportunity to visit the "seminary" in Wuppertal, where all Reformed ministerial candidates spend a year developing Reformed pastoral skills after finishing their theological studies at the universities. It is an excellent program. However, what stunned me there was that none of the students in that program expected to be able to work as a pastor after finishing the program. With the declining number of members in the churches and declining financial support, new ministers simply cannot be employed. This dynamic is causing great distress among those called to ministry and those in the churches. In North America, many of our churches, as they have lost members, have become focused on survival—and thus lost their passion for mission.

This loss of energy and spiritual vitality was recognized as a serious problem for Reformed churches from various parts of the world when we gathered for the 24th General Council (2004) in Accra. The spiritual energy, hospitality, and passion for mission that we found among Ghanaian Presbyterians was a wake-up call to many of us who have come to be known in our cultures as "God's frozen chosen." Out of this awareness, we adopted, for the first time in the history of the alliance (WARC), a major commitment to worship and spiritual renewal as a core calling and major program in our life together. We desperately need renewal in the power of the Holy Spirit, renewal that touches our souls, energizes our emotions, renews our worship and prayer life, and sends us out with a new excitement for Christ's mission.

Fragmentation of the Body of Christ

In 1552, in a letter to the English reformer Thomas Cranmer, the first Protestant Archbishop of Canterbury, John Calvin exclaimed that he would cross ten seas to promote the unity of the church. Unfortunately, Calvin's passion for the gift of communion and the unity of the church has not been replicated by many of his followers. For too many in the Reformed tradition, our movement has not only been about reformation (Calvin's intention) but has also become an excuse for fragmentation of the body of Christ.

A few years ago, when we were developing the Mission and Unity Project in WARC, Lukas Vischer did a study of Reformed divisions and found that of all the world's Christian traditions, none were as likely as the Reformed to divide the church. He found that we have 17 different Reformed churches in Nigeria, 84 in Korea, and more than anyone can count in the United States. In a church tradition where we are not bound together by a pope or bishop or by an understanding of the church controlling the integrity of the sacraments, we have found all kinds of (unbiblical) reasons to divide the church:

disagreements over theology or the interpretation of Scripture, ethnic divisions, immigration patterns, and power struggles between factions. And more often than not, when we divide once, it often is not long before the body that splits off divides again. We are just like the church in Corinth that Paul so powerfully exhorted: its members are the body of Christ and as such belong to one another. Our fragmentation weakens our witness when we cannot speak with one voice, leads us to distrust one another, and gives a negative witness to God's purposes of unity and reconciliation in the world.

A good example of this trend toward fragmentation is in my own country, where we have Presbyterian churches because the Scots organized them and Reformed churches because they were organized by the Dutch. Long beyond the time when Scottish or Dutch identity was influential or even reflected in our membership, we are still divided. We also have new denominations, like the Korean Presbyterian Church in America, growing out of more recent immigration. We certainly have many splits in the Presbyterian family growing out of differences in theology and biblical interpretation.

Another place where these divisions in the Reformed family are evident and are harming our Reformed witness is in Kenya. In 2008, following the electoral crisis in Kenya when it looked like ethnic violence might destroy that nation, I was asked by the World Council of Churches to lead a Living Letters Peacemaking delegation to visit and support reconciliation in that nation. One of the main reasons I was asked to lead that group is that one of the major fault lines cutting through the center of that crisis was between Presbyterian and Reformed Christians. I quickly discovered that, because of their respective mission histories, Presbyterians were in vast majority Kikuyus, and Reformed Christians were overwhelmingly Luos and Kalenjins. Presbyterians and Reformed were on opposite sides of the ethnic fault lines behind the killing and burning taking place in Kenya. Fortunately, those churches rose to the occasion and led in the cause of reconciliation, but how tragic that the ethnic divide that was threatening the nation was mirrored in how we had divided our Reformed family in Kenya into two communities. This is not the only place in the world where dividing Reformed Christians into separate churches based on their ethnicity has threatened the fabric of society, as the case of South Africa demonstrated so well.

God is indeed calling us as Reformed Christians to follow Jesus' last prayer in the Garden of Gethsemane that "they may all be one, . . . so that the world may believe" (John 17:21). From the local congregation to the national level to the world community, we are being called to reclaim our unity as Reformed Christians so that we might share in Christ's great plan for the reconciliation of the world. One of the great signs of hope in bringing together WARC and the Reformed Ecumenical Council is that we might model to the world and to our churches that God is calling us to unity and communion, and thus to a much more effective witness to God's peace and justice in the world.

Indeed, there are a number of good reasons to ask if the movement of Reformed churches has a vital future in our world. We must take seriously these realities that cause people, including our own, to question whether God still has a purpose and a ministry in store for Christians of the Reformed tradition.

Reasons to Believe in the Future of the Reformed Tradition

While there are great challenges facing our future as Reformed Christians, there are also great sources of strength among us. One of our greatest problems is that as we focus on our problems, we too rarely look to the strengths that God has given us as a source of inspiration and hope for our future.

A Theological Vision Second to None

The Calvin Jubilee has proved to be a time of blessing for the global Reformed community. The blessing has not primarily been because of the celebration of Calvin but rather because this has been a time in which the Reformed community has reclaimed its core values and its vision of our common calling. There has been far more interest in the Calvin Jubilee than I expected, and it has been very good for Reformed Christians.

I picked up a hint of this interest and enthusiasm three years ago when I visited with the presidents of the theological seminaries related to the National Presbyterian Church of Mexico. They felt that the Calvin Jubilee could be a defining moment for Mexican Presbyterians and expressed their hope that this would be a time when Reformed churches around the world would move forward with a Calvinist revolution in the twenty-first century. I was quite surprised when I first heard this suggestion. It was hard for me to think of any place more different from sixteenth-century Geneva than Mexico City in the twenty-first century. These colleagues knew well Calvin's shortcomings as well as his strengths. They ministered among a highly expressive, joyful people; yet after a global search, we in WARC were never able to find even one picture of Calvin smiling, to use in our Jubilee celebrations.

However, they were right, and this has been a time in which Reformed Christians have sought to reclaim their common ground in the Reformed faith. In Reformed churches around the world, there has been a high resonance for giving priority to three aspects of Calvin's legacy:

- His appreciation of the gift of community
- His commitment to justice in response to the sovereignty of God
- His passion for life and the creation

The core elements of Calvin's legacy are at the heart of our Reformed theology, which is life giving, is the source of our strength, and serves as the basis for faithful mission in our time. Among those core elements are the following:

- Making the word of God available to the people as the authoritative witness to Jesus Christ
- Building a church on the foundations of the Word and sacrament
- Caring for the well-being of the human community as our vocation
- Understanding that we have been elected to live our lives to the glory of God
- Organizing a community of shared leadership among ministers, elders, and the people of God in leading the church

These theological themes are at the heart of the gospel and are the life-giving foundations for Reformed Christians. This is a great strength for us all.

Leadership for God's Justice in the World

Reformed Christians know instinctively that we have been chosen by God to be about God's justice in the world. It is no accident that the major confessions of the twentieth century affirm so powerfully the power of God and the witness of Christ over against the forces of evil in our time. Barman, Belhar, and Accra are all Reformed confessions that articulate a clear stand for fullness of life and against the powers of evil found in Nazism, fascism, and apartheid. They make it clear that to stand against these evils is not only a social justice concern but also a matter of the integrity of the Christian faith and witness in our time.

Everywhere I have visited, I have found our member churches actively engaged in the struggle for justice, often at the risk of their own lives. I give thanks to God for the witness for justice, peace, and human rights through our churches in Colombia, in the Philippines, in Taiwan, in Romania, in the

Sudan, in South Africa, in Madagascar, in the Middle East, and in so many other parts of the world. I am delighted that through the alliance (WARC) we have been able to share in these courageous witnesses for justice.

On a global level, we have made a major contribution to the future of the world and to the church ecumenical by our joining together in Covenanting for Justice in the Economy and the Earth. The Accra Confession, which emerged from our last General Council yet is part of a long-term commitment of WARC to break the bonds of injustice, has often been controversial, but it speaks the truth, a truth that the world desperately needs to hear. This call to challenge the empire of our time to build an economic system that lessens rather than increases the gap between the rich and the poor, that ends grinding poverty for billions of people, and that creates a more just world—here is the heart of our calling. It is also a challenge for us to care for the earth, to stop its pollution and exploitation, and to care for those most negatively impacted with our abuse of the planet.

I am pleased that so many of our churches have affirmed the Accra Confession and joined in the Covenanting for Justice process. It is our signature commitment to the world. I am also pleased that we have been joined in this endeavor by ecumenical partners like the World Council of Churches, the Council for World Mission, and the Lutheran World Federation, for this is a concern that is truly ecumenical in nature. I am also gratified for so many regional efforts that have furthered this commitment and made it come alive.

If anything, the call of the Accra Confession is more urgent now than six years ago. Although many debated our strong actions in Accra, the global financial crisis and the exacerbation of global warming have shown to the world that we are right and reminded us all of how urgent this call remains in our time. It is a matter of great strength that Reformed Christians can be united in such a noble cause in our time. We are standing for something important!

An Inclusive People of God

Though our vision is sometimes ahead of our practice, more often than not the Reformed community has been in the leadership to make the church a truly inclusive community of Christ. We come from a tradition that from its earliest days has stood against hierarchy and exclusion and for the priesthood of all believers and shared leadership in the governance of the church, and we have particular challenges in our day to live out this Reformed principle. For the last twenty-five years, WARC has been strongly committed to a genuine partnership between women and men in the church. Efforts such as the Scholarship Program for Women from the global South have made a special contribution to this effort. This commitment has engaged us on the front lines of the struggle for gender justice, for the ordination of women, and for shared leadership across all barriers in the church.

Over the last quarter century, we have had a sea change in the reality of women being recognized for ordained leadership in our churches. While we still have a few churches that do not yet ordain women and many that do not yet have ordained women in equal numbers to men, the vast majority of our churches welcome both women and men to all ministries of the church. This is a major step forward and an important witness to the church ecumenical, embodying the promise of Galatians 3:28: "There is no longer Jew or Greek, there is no longer slave or free, there is no longer male and female; for all of you are one in Christ Jesus."

Following Calvin's example, Reformed churches in many of our countries have also sought to show signs of being an inclusive community in many other ways. Like Calvin in Geneva, many of our churches have welcomed immigrants, worked for justice for immigrants, and sought ways to welcome immigrants from other cultures into the life of our churches. We have also continued the struggle to break down barriers of race and class in the Christian community. The growing number of churches in our fellowship that are embracing the Belhar Confession and its call to eschew racism in the life of the church and society is a real sign of hope.

Though we are still divided on how we view sexual orientation in our commitment to building an inclusive community, we have seen many in our fellowship welcome people into leadership in their churches regardless of sexual orientation, and we have all shared the commitment to stand together for human rights for all people, whatever their sexual orientation.

As a community that over the last six years has sought to allow Jesus' promise "that all might have life in fullness" (John 10:10 alt.; our theme in Accra) to come alive in and among us, Reformed churches are in many places at the forefront of a movement to transform our congregations into truly inclusive communities of Christ. This is another strength, not unique to Reformed churches, but very much part of our ethos and our future.

Reformed, Therefore Ecumenical

One of our great strengths is what we do not claim to be: *the* church. As Reformed Christians, we know in our souls that we are only one part of the church: we cannot be whole, or faithful to Jesus Christ, unless we seek to restore the unity and wholeness of Christ's church. Because of that commitment, we have always invited all baptized Christians to join us at the Lord's Table and have always recognized their baptisms.

Some years ago, Robert McAfee Brown wrote an article for the *Presbyterian Survey* in which he summed up our ecumenical commitment: "I am Reformed; therefore, I am ecumenical." To be Reformed, according to Brown, is by its very nature to be ecumenical. From its very beginning, WARC has seen itself not as an end in itself but as part of a broader ecumenical movement. That is why our churches have always been leaders in the World Council of Churches, in their National Councils of Churches, and in all major efforts for Christian unity. We have also been churches that have naturally entered into union with other churches, and today we count among our members in WARC a good number of national churches that are actually union churches. It is no accident that so many of the great ecumenical leaders have arisen from the Reformed tradition.

We live in a time in which unity and reconciliation with other religious communities (both Christian and other faith) is urgent for the peace of the world. At the beginning of the twenty-first century, most of our major wars and conflicts are occurring at the confluence of ethnic and religious conflict, which makes our propensity to be ecumenical and to pursue reconciliation with people of other faiths all the more urgent. This is how we carry out our programs in WARC, and it is a great strength that I have seen at work in our member churches in all parts of the world.

Vital Christian Communities

While our theological vision, our commitment to justice, our struggle to be inclusive communities, and our Reformed propensity for ecumenism are sources of great strength and hope for our future, our greatest strength is in our hundreds of thousands of congregations, where the gospel is proclaimed, the sacraments are celebrated, the community is nurtured, and the people are going forth in mission. I have had the privilege of being in hundreds of those congregations in all parts of the world; with few exceptions, I have had my faith in Christ strengthened as I have been in these communities, where the signs of the Holy Spirit are abundant. Friends, our churches are alive with the gospel of Jesus Christ, and that is our greatest strength.

The most important part of my personal spiritual journey has been the opportunity on many occasions (especially in the global South) to be with congregations in settings (like Sudan, Pakistan, or Cuba) where there was great suffering and the very fabric of human life seemed to be at risk. Yet in these very places I was welcomed as a brother in Christ; I found among these people, who seemed to have no good reason to believe in the goodness of God, a faith in Christ and a spiritual presence that I could not understand but for which I could only give thanks to God. Those situations made me know that the suffering love of Christ really is the most powerful thing in the world. These experiences brought me closer to God and are some of the greatest gifts I have ever received. It also renewed my commitment to be one in Christ with these brothers and sisters and to join them in a mission so that no one would need to live in a situation where one might question whether there is reason to believe in the goodness of God.

It is amazing how different our hundreds of thousands of congregations are from one another yet how, even in their diversity, they show the strengths of the Reformed tradition in their life and witness. Churches as different as the Yolo Church in Kinshasa, Congo; the Presbyterian Church in Lar in the Sudan; the Myung Sung Presbyterian Church in Seoul, Korea; the women's church among the Maya Quiche Indians in Guatemala; the First Presbyterian Church in Havana; the Great Church in Debrecen, Hungary; and my local congregation, Springdale Presbyterian Church in Louisville, Kentucky—all seem, on the surface, to have hardly anything in common. But if you probe a little more deeply, you will find that they all share a love for Christ and neighbor, a vision of the best dreams of Calvin, a commitment to justice, a sense of being an inclusive and welcoming community, an ecumenical spirit, and a place where the Holy Spirit is at work among the people. The same could be said of thousands of other congregations in our fellowship.

Conclusion

We are at a turning point in the Reformed tradition. In Grand Rapids we will be launching a new chapter in our life together as we become the World Communion of Reformed Churches. At the same time, we have reached an important historical milestone, the 500th anniversary of our movement. This is the time for us to claim the best of our heritage and to be open to the radical new things that God may have in store for us in the years ahead.

I believe that there is a future—a vital and exciting future—for the Reformed movement in the twenty-first century. However, we cannot overlook too easily that there are serious problems in our common life that we must address with repentance and commitment to change. God does intend for us to master the technology, culture, and ethos of our time as we reach out to a new generation. God intends for our churches to be vital and growing churches. And God surely intends for us to give up our divisive and fragmenting ways and join the movement for unity and reconciliation in the church and the world.

As we do that, we have major strengths and resources in our life together that we need to celebrate and reclaim and that can give us the strength for "turning the world upside down" (Acts 17:6) for the gospel in our time:

- A theological vision, growing out of Calvin's legacy, that is second to none
- Leadership for God's justice in the world as part of our Reformed DNA
- A desire to be a truly inclusive and welcoming community of all of God's people
- An ecumenical spirit that seeks reconciliation with all people of faith
- Thousands of vital congregations, where the gospel is preached, the sacraments are administered, the community is nurtured, and the people are going forth in mission

It is critical that we address our shortcomings and build upon our strengths for the future of our Reformed movement worldwide: that is exactly what I believe God intends for us to do. I want to close by illustrating that through an insight I gained from one of the books that impacted me most in my early walk with Christ. It was the little volume by C. S. Lewis titled *The Screwtape Letters*. In this book, the character Screwtape (the devil) writes letters to his agent, Wormwood, about how to tempt Christians and draw them away from God's work so that Screwtape can have his way in the world. What struck me when I read again these fictional letters was how the vast majority of the strategies that Screwtape proposes to Wormwood are, in one way or another, strategies to make Christians doubt themselves, focus on their shortcomings, and distrust their fellow Christians—and never build on the strengths that are at the heart of our community. For Screwtape, it is clear that if Wormwood can do that, the devil could have a field day.

Friends, I think we in the world Reformed community are being called to say a loud and strong *no* to Screwtape, Wormwood, and all of their contemporary colleagues; we are called to reclaim our unity in Christ and our confidence in God and one another. We have challenges to face, but God has given us incredible gifts and strengths in the World Communion of Reformed Churches on which to build, and we need to be doing just that—building on these great gifts of our Reformed tradition and reality to shape our churches for the twenty-first century, truly being "'churches reformed, always reforming,' according to the Word of God and the call of the Spirit."

Appendix 1

Biographical Outline of Clifton Kirkpatrick

Professional Ministry Experience

Stated Clerk of the General Assembly, Presbyterian Church (U.S.A.), 1996 to present

Director, Worldwide Ministries Division, Presbyterian Church (U.S.A.), 1993–96

Director, Global Mission Ministry Unit, Presbyterian Church (U.S.A.), 1987–93

Director, Division of International Mission, General Assembly Mission Board, Presbyterian Church U.S., 1981–87

Executive Director, Houston Metropolitan Ministries, 1972–81

Executive Director, Fort Worth Area Council of Churches, 1969–72

Chief Executive for the agency for cooperation and service for 127 Protestant and Catholic churches in Tarrant County, Texas

Assistant Director, Greater Dallas Council of Churches, 1968–69

Assistant to the Chief Executive for the metropolitan ecumenical agency of Dallas, Texas

Formal Education

Davidson (North Carolina) College, Bachelor of Arts Degree, 1966

Yale University, Master of Divinity Degree, 1968

Harvard University, Merrill Fellow (postgraduate fellowship award), Spring term, 1975

McCormick Theological Seminary, Doctor of Ministry Degree, 1981

Honorary Degrees

Westminster (Pennsylvania) College, Doctor of Divinity Degree, 1990
Hannam University (Korea), Doctor of Literature Degree, 1995
Silliman University (Philippines), Doctor of Humanities, 2001

Service to the Wider Church

Presbyterian Church (USA) General Assembly

Commissioner, 1978 General Assembly, Presbyterian Church U.S.
Corresponding Member of every General Assembly of the Presbyterian Church (U.S.A.)
Member, General Assembly Committee on Ecumenical Relations
Member, Moderator's Special Committee on Reconciliation with the Presbyterian Lay Committee
Member and Secretary, Board of Trustees, Presbyterian Church (U.S.A.) Foundation
Corresponding Member and Recording Secretary, General Assembly Council
Member, Committee for the Presbyterian Historical Society
Member, Special Committee on the Consultation on Church Union

National Council of Churches of Christ in the U.S.A.

Member of the General Assembly and Executive Committee
Member of the Board of Directors, Church World Service
Executive Committee Member and former Chair of Division of Overseas Ministries

World Council of Churches

Member of the Executive and Central Committees
Commission Member, Commission on World Mission and Evangelism
Delegate to Seventh Assembly, Canberra, 1991; Eighth Assembly, Harare, 1998; and Ninth Assembly, Porto Alegre, 2006
General Secretary Search Committee (2002–2003)

World Alliance of Reformed Churches

President, 2004–2010

Member of the General Council, Seoul, Korea, 1989; and Debrecen, Hungary, 1997
Member of Mission in Unity Project Committee
Executive Committee Member

Other

Board of Trustees, National Interfaith Cable Coalition
Council of Presidents, United States Chapter of the World Conference on Religion and Peace
Minister Member of New Covenant Presbytery
Member, Association of Stated Clerks
Life Member and Past President, National Association of Ecumenical Staff

Personal and Civic

Married to Diane Worthington Kirkpatrick, Director of Habitat for Humanity of Louisville
Two children: Elizabeth, pastor of the Graniteville (Vermont) Presbyterian Church; and David, working in wind energy development in Tehachapi, California
One grandchild: Katherine Elizabeth Brucken, two years old (in 2009) and absolutely beautiful!
Active participant and affiliate member, Springdale Presbyterian Church, Louisville, Kentucky
Member, Advisory Committee, Americans United for Humanitarian Trade with Cuba
Chair of Successful School Age Youth Community Investment Team
Member of the Cabinet, United Way of Metro Louisville
Coauthor with William H. Hopper Jr., *What Unites Presbyterians: Common Ground for Troubled Times* (Louisville, KY: Geneva Press, 1997)

Appendix 2

The Accra Confession

Covenanting for Justice in the Economy and the Earth

Introduction

1. In response to the urgent call of the Southern African constituency which met in Kitwe in 1995 and in recognition of the increasing urgency of global economic injustice and ecological destruction, the 23rd General Council (Debrecen, Hungary, 1997) invited the member churches of the World Alliance of Reformed Churches to enter into a process of "recognition, education, and confession (*processus confessionis*)." The churches reflected on the text of Isaiah 58.6, ". . . break the chains of oppression and the yoke of injustice, and let the oppressed go free," as they heard the cries of brothers and sisters around the world and witnessed God's gift of creation under threat.

2. Since then, nine member churches have committed themselves to a faith stance; some are in the process of covenanting; and others have studied the issues and come to a recognition of the depth of the crisis. Further, in partnership with the World Council of Churches, the Lutheran World Federation and regional ecumenical organizations, the World Alliance of Reformed Churches has engaged in consultations in all regions of the world, from Seoul/Bangkok (1999) to Stony Point (2004). Additional consultations took place with churches from the South in Buenos Aires (2003) and with churches from South and North in London Colney (2004).

3. Gathered in Accra, Ghana, for the General Council of the World Alliance of Reformed Churches, we visited the slave dungeons of Elmina and Cape Coast where millions of Africans were commodified, sold and subjected to the

The Accra Confession (2004), at http://warc.jalb.de/warcajsp/side.jsp?news_id=1157&navi=45.

166

horrors of repression and death. The cries of "never again" are put to the lie by the ongoing realities of human trafficking and the oppression of the global economic system.

4. Today we come to take a decision of faith commitment.

Reading the signs of the times

5. We have heard that creation continues to groan, in bondage, waiting for its liberation (Rom 8.22). We are challenged by the cries of the people who suffer and by the woundedness of creation itself. We see a dramatic convergence between the suffering of the people and the damage done to the rest of creation.

6. The signs of the times have become more alarming and must be interpreted. The root causes of massive threats to life are above all the product of an unjust economic system defended and protected by political and military might. Economic systems are a matter of life or death.

7. We live in a scandalous world that denies God's call to life for all. The annual income of the richest 1 per cent is equal to that of the poorest 57 per cent, and 24,000 people die each day from poverty and malnutrition. The debt of poor countries continues to increase despite paying back their original borrowing many times over. Resource-driven wars claim the lives of millions, while millions more die of preventable diseases. The HIV and AIDS global pandemic afflicts life in all parts of the world, affecting the poorest where generic drugs are not available. The majority of those in poverty are women and children[,] and the number of people living in absolute poverty on less than one US dollar per day continues to increase.

8. The policy of unlimited growth among industrialized countries and the drive for profit of transnational corporations have plundered the earth and severely damaged the environment. In 1989, one species disappeared each day and by 2000 it was one every hour. Climate change, the depletion of fish stocks, deforestation, soil erosion, and threats to fresh water are among the devastating consequences. Communities are disrupted, livelihoods are lost, coastal regions and Pacific islands are threatened with inundation, and storms increase. High levels of radioactivity threaten health and ecology. Life forms and cultural knowledge are being patented for financial gain.

9. This crisis is directly related to the development of neoliberal economic globalization, which is based on the following beliefs:

   • unrestrained competition, consumerism and the unlimited economic growth and accumulation of wealth are the best for the whole world;
   • the ownership of private property has no social obligation;

- capital speculation, liberalization and deregulation of the market, privatization of public utilities and national resources, unrestricted access for foreign
investments and imports, lower taxes and the unrestricted movement of
capital will achieve wealth for all;
- social obligations, protection of the poor and the weak, trade unions, and
relationships between people, are subordinate to the processes of economic
growth and capital accumulation.

10. This is an ideology that claims to be without alternative, demanding an endless
flow of sacrifices from the poor and creation. It makes the false promise
that it can save the world through the creation of wealth and prosperity,
claiming sovereignty over life and demanding total allegiance which amounts
to idolatry.

11. We recognize the enormity and complexity of the situation. We do not seek
simple answers. As seekers of truth and justice and looking through the eyes
of powerless and suffering people, we see that the current world (dis)order is
rooted in an extremely complex and immoral economic system defended by
empire. In using the term "empire" we mean the coming together of economic,
cultural, political and military power that constitutes a system of domination
led by powerful nations to protect and defend their own interests.

12. In classical liberal economics, the state exists to protect private property
and contracts in the competitive market. Through the struggles of the labour
movement, states began to regulate markets and provide for the welfare of
people. Since the 1980s, through the transnationalization of capital, neoliberalism has set out to dismantle the welfare functions of the state. Under
neoliberalism the purpose of the economy is to increase profits and return for
the owners of production and financial capital, while excluding the majority
of the people and treating nature as a commodity.

13. As markets have become global so have the political and legal institutions which protect them. The government of the United States of America
and its allies, together with international finance and trade institutions
(International Monetary Fund, World Bank, World Trade Organization) use
political, economic or military alliances to protect and advance the interest
of capital owners.

14. We see the dramatic convergence of the economic crisis with the integration
of economic globalization and geopolitics backed by neoliberal ideology.
This is a global system that defends and protects the interests of the powerful.
It affects and captivates us all. Further, in biblical terms such a system of
wealth accumulation at the expense of the poor is seen as unfaithful to God
and responsible for preventable human suffering and is called Mammon. Jesus
has told us that we cannot serve both God and Mammon (Lk 16.13).

Confession of faith in the face of economic injustice and ecological destruction

15. Faith commitment may be expressed in various ways according to regional and theological traditions: as confession, as confessing together, as faith stance, as being faithful to the covenant of God. We choose confession, not meaning a classical doctrinal confession, because the World Alliance of Reformed Churches cannot make such a confession, but to show the necessity and urgency of an active response to the challenges of our time and the call of Debrecen. We invite member churches to receive and respond to our common witness.

16. Speaking from our Reformed tradition and having read the signs of the times, the General Council of the World Alliance of Reformed Churches affirms that global economic justice is essential to the integrity of our faith in God and our discipleship as Christians. We believe that the integrity of our faith is at stake if we remain silent or refuse to act in the face of the current system of neoliberal economic globalization and therefore we confess before God and one another.

17. We believe in God, Creator and Sustainer of all life, who calls us as partners in the creation and redemption of the world. We live under the promise that Jesus Christ came so that all might have life in fullness (Jn 10.10). Guided and upheld by the Holy Spirit we open ourselves to the reality of our world.

18. We believe that God is sovereign over all creation. "The earth is the Lord's and the fullness thereof" (Ps 24.1).

19. Therefore, we reject the current world economic order imposed by global neoliberal capitalism and any other economic system, including absolute planned economies, which defy God's covenant by excluding the poor, the vulnerable and the whole of creation from the fullness of life. We reject any claim of economic, political and military empire which subverts God's sovereignty over life and acts contrary to God's just rule.

20. We believe that God has made a covenant with all of creation (Gen 9.8–12). God has brought into being an earth community based on the vision of justice and peace. The covenant is a gift of grace that is not for sale in the market place (Is 55.1). It is an economy of grace for the household of all of creation. Jesus shows that this is an inclusive covenant in which the poor and marginalized are preferential partners and calls us to put justice for the "least of these" (Mt 25.40) at the centre of the community of life. All creation is blessed and included in this covenant (Hos 2.18ff.).

21. Therefore we reject the culture of rampant consumerism and the competitive greed and selfishness of the neoliberal global market system or any other system which claims there is no alternative.

22. We believe that any economy of the household of life given to us by God's covenant to sustain life is accountable to God. We believe the economy exists to serve the dignity and well-being of people in community, within the bounds of the sustainability of creation. We believe that human beings are called to choose God over Mammon and that confessing our faith is an act of obedience.

23. Therefore we reject the unregulated accumulation of wealth and limitless growth that has already cost the lives of millions and destroyed much of God's creation.

24. We believe that God is a God of justice. In a world of corruption, exploitation and greed, God is in a special way the God of the destitute, the poor, the exploited, the wronged and the abused (Ps 146.7–9). God calls for just relationships with all creation.

25. Therefore we reject any ideology or economic regime that puts profits before people, does not care for all creation and privatizes those gifts of God meant for all. We reject any teaching which justifies those who support, or fail to resist, such an ideology in the name of the gospel.

26. We believe that God calls us to stand with those who are victims of injustice. We know what the Lord requires of us: to do justice, love kindness, and walk in God's way (Mic 6.8). We are called to stand against any form of injustice in the economy and the destruction of the environment, "so that justice may roll down like waters, and righteousness like an ever-flowing stream" (Am 5.24).

27. Therefore we reject any theology that claims that God is only with the rich and that poverty is the fault of the poor. We reject any form of injustice which destroys right relations—gender, race, class, disability, or caste. We reject any theology which affirms that human interests dominate nature.

28. We believe that God calls us to hear the cries of the poor and the groaning of creation and to follow the public mission of Jesus Christ[,] who came so that all may have life and have it in fullness (Jn 10.10). Jesus brings justice to the oppressed and gives bread to the hungry; he frees the prisoner and restores sight to the blind (Lk 4.18); he supports and protects the downtrodden, the stranger, the orphans and the widows.

29. Therefore we reject any church practice or teaching which excludes the poor and care for creation, in its mission; giving comfort to those who come to "steal, kill and destroy" (Jn 10.10) rather than following the "Good Shepherd" who has come for life for all (Jn 10.11).

30. We believe that God calls men, women and children from every place together, rich and poor, to uphold the unity of the church and its mission so that the reconciliation to which Christ calls can become visible.

31. Therefore we reject any attempt in the life of the church to separate justice and unity.

32. We believe that we are called in the Spirit to account for the hope that is within us through Jesus Christ and believe that justice shall prevail and peace shall reign.
33. We commit ourselves to seek a global covenant for justice in the economy and the earth in the household of God.
34. We humbly confess this hope, knowing that we, too, stand under the judgement of God's justice.

   • We acknowledge the complicity and guilt of those who consciously or unconsciously benefit from the current neoliberal economic global system; we recognize that this includes both churches and members of our own Reformed family and therefore we call for confession of sin.
   • We acknowledge that we have become captivated by the culture of consumerism and the competitive greed and selfishness of the current economic system. This has all too often permeated our very spirituality.
   • We confess our sin in misusing creation and failing to play our role as stewards and companions of nature.
   • We confess our sin that our disunity within the Reformed family has impaired our ability to serve God's mission in fullness.

35. We believe in obedience to Jesus Christ, that the church is called to confess, witness and act, even though the authorities and human law might forbid them, and punishment and suffering be the consequence (Acts 4.18ff.). Jesus is Lord.
36. We join in praise to God, Creator, Redeemer, Spirit, who has "brought down the mighty from their thrones, lifted up the lowly, filled the hungry with good things and sent the rich away with empty hands" (Lk 1.52f.).

Covenanting for Justice

37. By confessing our faith together, we covenant in obedience to God's will as an act of faithfulness in mutual solidarity and in accountable relationships. This binds us together to work for justice in the economy and the earth both in our common global context as well as our various regional and local settings.
38. On this common journey, some churches have already expressed their commitment in a confession of faith. We urge them to continue to translate this confession into concrete actions both regionally and locally. Other churches have already begun to engage in this process, including taking actions[,] and we urge them to engage further, through education, confession and action. To those other churches, which are still in the process of recognition, we urge

them on the basis of our mutual covenanting accountability, to deepen their education and move forward towards confession.

39. The General Council calls upon member churches, on the basis of this covenanting relationship, to undertake the difficult and prophetic task of interpreting this confession to their local congregations.

40. The General Council urges member churches to implement this confession by following up the Public Issues Committee's recommendations on economic justice and ecological issues (see Appendix 18).

41. The General Council commits the World Alliance of Reformed Churches to work together with other communions, the ecumenical community, the community of other faiths, civil movements and people's movements for a just economy and the integrity of creation and calls upon our member churches to do the same.

42. Now we proclaim with passion that we will commit ourselves, our time and our energy to changing, renewing and restoring the economy and the earth, choosing life, so that we and our descendants might live (Deut 30.19).

Notes

EDITOR'S PREFACE

1. At http://www.ccel.org/ccel/calvin/calcom35.vii.v.html.

CHAPTER 1: *KOINŌNIA* AND MISSION

1. The REC published a series of articles in the 1990s: Eddie Bruwer, "Poverty, Dependency and Liberating Development"; J. J. Kritzinger, "Church and Society in Development Ministries"; and Samuel Mbambo, "How Does the Rich Church Relate to the Poor?" in *REC Mission Bulletin* 16, nos. 3–4 (October 1996): 4–52. See also Richard L. van Houten, "Sharing Resources in the REC," *REC Mission Bulletin* 17, no. 2 (July 1997): 2–13; J. J. Kritzinger, "Dependency and Independence," *REC Mission Bulletin* 20, no. 2 (June 2000): 4–11; Richard L. van Houten, "Gifts, Needs, Sharing and Relationships: A Review Essay on the Mennonite World Conference Study *Sharing Gifts in the Global Family of Faith*," *REC Focus* 3, no. 4 (December 2003): 39–41.

2. In 2000 the REC Assembly suggested that the REC explore the notion of partnership. We (the REC) published a provocative article by Roland Hoksbergen, "Partnering for Development: Why It's So Important, Why It's So Hard, How to Go about It," *REC Focus* 3, no. 4 (December 2003): 3–21. We spent some discussion time at our 2005 Assembly, with a lead speech by Gideon van der Watt, "Sharing in Partnership (*Koinōnia*): A Conversation Starter," *REC Focus* 5, nos. 3–4 (December 2005): 4–11.

3. Hoksbergen, "Partnering for Development," 3–21.

CHAPTER 3: THE JOY OF GROWING OLD

1. Rubem Alves, "Quiero vivir muchos años," in *Tempo e Presença*, Rio de Janeiro, 1996.

2. Elizabeth Schüssler Fiorenza, *Los caminos de la sabiduría: Una introducción a la feminista interpretación de la Biblia* (Santander, Spain: Sal Térrae, 2004), 181.

3. See the description of these fundamental elements of Wisdom in Elizabeth A. Johnson, *She Who Is: The Mystery of God in Feminist Theological Discourse* (New York: Crossroad, 1992), 165–66.

4. Sharon H. Ringe, *Wisdom's Friends: Community and Christology in the Fourth Gospel* (Louisville, KY: Westminster John Knox Press, 1999), 31.

5. This text is inspired by Prov. 8:1–15, as given by Elizabeth Schüssler Fiorenza in her book *Pero Ella Dijo: Prácticas feministas de interpretación bíblica* (Madrid: Trotta, 1996), 31.

CHAPTER 5: FUNDING AND FAITHFULNESS

1. Trevor Grundy, "Archbishop of Canterbury Quotes Marx on 'Unbridled Capitalism,'" ENI-08-0768, September 25, 2008, http://egliseepiscopal.org/78650_101060_ENG_HTM .htm. Also see "Church Finance Role Questioned after Leaders Slam Markets," ENI-08-0781, September 29, 2008, http://www.christiantelegraph.com/issue3253.html. (ENI = Ecumenical News International.)

2. I am indebted to the broader definition of Charles Maier, who defines political economy as an approach that "interrogates economic doctrines to disclose their sociological and political premises. . . . In sum, [it] regards economic ideas and behavior not as frameworks for analysis, but as beliefs and actions that must themselves be explained. " See Charles S. Mayer, *In Search of Stability: Explorations in Historical Political Economy* (Cambridge: Cambridge University Press, 1987), 3–6.

3. See Robert Gilpin, *The Political Economy of International Relations* (Princeton, NJ: Princeton University Press, 1987).

4. See my *Partnership, Solidarity, and Mission: Transforming Structures in Mission*, A study paper for the Presbyterian Church (U.S.A.) (Louisville, KY: Worldwide Ministries Division, 2003).

CHAPTER 7: WHEN MISSION AND JUSTICE EMBRACE

1. Alex de Waal, *Famine Crimes: Politics and the Disaster Relief Industry in Africa* (Bloomington: Indiana University Press, in association with African Rights and the International African Institute, 1997), 127.

2. WARC and the John Knox International Reformed Center, *The Legacy of John Calvin: Some Actions for the Church in the 21st Century*, ed. Setri Nyomi (Geneva: WARC, 2008), 28–31.

3. This enduring legacy of division and conflict occasioned by differing emphases on two critically important aspects of mission, evangelism and justice, appears to be diminishing as a younger generation insists on the relevance of issues of poverty and the environment to their faith. In this sense, *Mission and Evangelism: An Ecumenical Affirmation,* produced by the WCC in 1982, was prescient: "There is no evangelism without solidarity; there is no Christian solidarity that does not involve sharing the knowledge of the kingdom which is God's promise to the poor of the earth" (¶ 34).

4. David Dawson, "A Mission Funding System for the 21st Century," electronically published summary of the monograph, produced for the Yale-Edinburgh Group on the History of the Missionary Movement and Non-Western Christianity, 2004, http://www.shenango.org/ PDF/Dawson/Yale-Edinburgh%202004-online.pdf.

5. Scott W. Sunquist and Caroline N. Becker, *A History of Presbyterian Missions, 1944– 2007* (Louisville, KY: Geneva Press, 2008), 61.

6. "Partnership in mission involves two or more organizations who agree to submit themselves to a common task or goal, mutually giving and receiving and surrounded by prayer

so that God's work can be more faithfully accomplished. Theologically and biblically, partnership is based on the fundamental belief that God's love for the world is greater than any one church can possibly comprehend or realize." PC(USA), "Presbyterians Do Mission in Partnership," policy statement adopted by the General Assembly, 2003, https://www.pcusa.org/worldwide/get-involved/partnership.htm.

7. At http://www.reuters.com/article/companyNewsAndPR/idUSN2626993520090326.

8. At http://www.christianitytoday.com/ct/2007/april/37.70.html.

CHAPTER 11: THE POLITICS OF POWER

1. Bread for the World, "Hunger Facts—International," http://www.bread.org/learn/hunger-basics/hunger-facts-international.html.

2. I do not mean to imply that it is only Reformed Christians who recognize poverty as a travesty of justice! However, my remarks in this volume are focused on ways in which the Reformed community has responded to the issues and problems of economic injustice in the late 20th and early 21st centuries.

3. The Accra Confession, ¶ 11 (in an appendix, below).

4. Some prominent theologians and church leaders in the global North share the ideological critique of neoliberal economics that is represented in the Accra Confession, some of whom have participated as allies with the churches from the global South in processes leading up to and following the 24th General Council. Some other theologians and church leaders in the global North agree ideologically and theologically with Accra, but caution that a different approach is necessary if we wish to gain the broad support of the churches in the global North.

5. For a more detailed examination of these tensions and issues, see the World Council of Churches Faith and Order case study on WARC and the Accra Confession, which is part of their new study on Moral Discernment in the Churches.

6. The Barmen Declaration (1934) denounced the German church's collusion with Nazi Germany; likewise, the Belhar Confession (1986) denounced participation in the apartheid system of South African as a violation of the unity of the church.

CHAPTER 12: THE KING IS NAKED

1. For a recent discussion and description of "empire" from a global South perspective, see for instance, "An Ecumenical Faith Stance Against Global Empire. For a Liberated Earth Community. Manila, Philippines, July 2006," http://warc.jalb.de/warcajsp/side.jsp?news_id=1166&navi=45.

CHAPTER 13: LIVING FAITHFULLY IN THE CONTEXT OF EMPIRE

1. Report to the United Church of Canada General Council 40, August 2009: "Covenanting to Live Faithfully in the Midst of Empire."

2. Ibid., 2.

3. World Alliance of Reformed Churches General Assembly, Accra, Ghana, 2004.

4. Minutes, the Executive of the General Council, October 29–November 1, 2004, Toronto.

5. Mission Section Plenary Report, 24th General Assembly of the World Alliance of Reformed Churches (WARC), Accra, Ghana, October 2004.

6. Assembly Documents, 9th General Assembly of the World Council of Churches, Porto Alegre, Brazil, 2006.

7. The New Testament offers several but similar perspectives on *kairos*: the Greek means "the right or opportune time." For example, in Luke 12:54–56, *kairos* is extraordinary time, requiring interpretation. The capacity to read the signs of the times, the *kairos*, and respond is an issue of faith; Rom. 13:11–13 says that *kairos* time is here now. It calls for action, conversion, and transformation—a change of life; 2 Cor. 6:1–2 treats *kairos* as not just crisis but also opportunity and favor. God assists us in discerning the *kairos*—a moment of grace. Source: http://www.kairoscanada.org/e/network/KairosBibleStudy.pdf.

8. Letter to Prime Minister Harper [Ottawa] re Forthcoming G-20 meeting, from the Halifax Initiative Coalition and other parties, March 26, 2009, http://www.foecanada.org/images/stories/pdfs/harper_pre_g-20_meeting_march_09_final.pdf.

9. A Song of Faith, United Church of Canada, 2006.

10. See Appendix of A Covenant for Life in Creation.

11. Here insert names of groups within your community, in Canada, and globally who are exploited by forms of empire and with whom your group or congregation is seeking to build right relationships.

CHAPTER 14: A GIFT FROM ISLAM

1. At http://www.acommonword.com/.

2. PBUH stands for "Peace Be Upon Him," the salutation offered to any prophet of Islam.

3. At http://www.archbishopofcanterbury.org/1892.

4. At http://www.archbishopofcanterbury.org/2005.

CHAPTER 15: THE BODY LIES BLEEDING

1. "Sadoleto's Letter to the Genevans," in *A Reformation Debate*, ed. John C. Olin (New York: Fordham University Press, 2000), 40.

2. "Calvin's Reply to Sadoleto," in *A Reformation Debate*, 87.

3. Calvin, "Letter to Cranmer" (1552), in *Selected Works of John Calvin: Tracts and Letters*, ed. Henry Beveridge and Jules Bonnet, vol. 5, *Letters*, pt. 2, *1545–1553*, trans. David Constable (Edinburgh: Calvin Translation Society, 1844–58; reprinted, Grand Rapids: Baker Book House, 1954), 355.

4. Calvin, "Letter to the Reformed Churches of France" (1560), in *Tracts and Letters*, vol. 7, *Letters*, pt. 4, *1559–1564*, trans. M. R. Gilchrist, 168–70.

5. Calvin, commentary on Eph. 4:4 in *Commentaries on the Epistles of Paul to the Galatians and Ephesians*, trans. William Pringle (Grand Rapids: Baker Book House, 1993), 268.

6. Ephraim Radner, *The End of the Church* (Grand Rapids: Wm. B. Eerdmans Publishing Co., 1998), 277.

7. Ingolf Dalferth, "I Determine What God Is!" *Theology Today* 57, no. 1 (April 2000).

8. Bruce Marshall, "The Disunity of the Church and the Credibility of the Gospel," *Theology Today* 50, no. 1 (April 1993): 82.

9. *The Christian Century* 126, no. 7 (April 7, 2009), 15.

10. Groupe des Dombes, *For the Conversion of the Churches* (Geneva: WCC Publications, 1993), 28.

11. Carl E. Braaten and Robert W. Jenson, eds., *In One Body through the Cross* (Grand Rapids: Wm. B. Eerdmans Publishing Co., 2003), 57–58.

12. John Paul II, *Ut Unum Sint* (Washington, DC: United States Catholic Conference, 1995, Publication 5-050), ¶ 15, p. 20; also at http://www.vatican.va/edocs/ENG0221/_P4.HTM.

CHAPTER 16: REFLECTIONS ON ECUMENISM IN THE CALVIN YEAR

1. Calvin, *Institutes of the Christian Religion*, ed. John T. McNeill, trans. Ford Lewis Battles, 2 vols., Library of Christian Classics 21–22 (Philadelphia: Westminster Press, 1960), 4.1.9 (2:1023).

2. Lukas Vischer, *Pia Conspiratio: Calvin's Commitment to the Unity of Christ's Church*, reprinted as *Theology and Worship Occasional Paper No. 20* (Louisville, KY: Presbyterian Church (U.S.A.), 2007), 28. Vischer has brought together many key passages from Calvin on the unity of the church.

3. *Institutes* 3.7.6 alt. (1:696).

4. *Institutes* 4.17.38 (2:1415).

CHAPTER 17: THE ECUMENICAL STANCE OF THE PC(USA)

1. At http://www.pcusa.org/ecumenicalrelations/resources/ecumenical-stance-of-the-pcusa.pdf.

2. Jonathan Sacks has rightly observed that there is no difference so small that it cannot, under pressure, be turned into a marker of identity and an occasion for estrangement. What we do with differences is the central matter. *The Dignity of Difference: How to Avoid the Clash of Civilizations* (London: Continuum, 2002), 4.

3. Peter Hodgson, *Revisioning the Church: Ecclesial Freedom in the New Paradigm* (Philadelphia: Fortress Press, 1988), 39.

4. Ibid., 103.

5. *The Constitution of the Presbyterian Church (U.S.A.)*, Part I, *Book of Confessions* (Louisville, KY: Office of the General Assembly, 1999), §5.126.

6. *Third World Conference on Faith and Order: Held at Lund, August 15th–19th, 1952*, ed. Oliver S. Tomkins (London: SCM, 1953), 15–16.

7. Sacks, *The Dignity of Difference*, 4.

CHAPTER 18: CHRISTIAN UNITY IN THE 21ST CENTURY

1. Michael Kinnamon, *Truth and Community: Diversity and Its Limits in the Ecumenical Movement* (Grand Rapids: Wm. B. Eerdmans Publishing Co., 1988), viii.

2. Keith F. Nickle and Timothy F. Lull, *A Common Calling: The Witness of Our Reformation Churches in North America Today* (Minneapolis: Fortress Press, 1993), 25.

CHAPTER 19: UNITY: GIFT AND DEMAND

1. Calvin, *Tracts and Letters*, vol. 5, pt. 2, 345ff.

2. Adelle M. Banks, "U.S. Churches that Split Over Race to Worship in Philadelphia," *DisciplesWorld* (October 13, 2009), http://www.disciplesworld.com/newsArticle.html?wsnID=15957

CHAPTER 21: THE ECUMENICAL SIGNIFICANCE OF THE WCRC

1. Philip Jenkins, *The Next Christendom: The Coming of Global Christianity* (Oxford: Oxford University Press, 2002), 3.

CHAPTER 24: ECUMENICAL FORMATION FROM A LAYPERSON'S PERSPECTIVE

1. Pew Forum on Religion and Public Life, "U.S. Religious Landscape Survey—Religious Affiliation: Diverse and Dynamic," February 2008, http://pewresearch.org/pubs/743/

united-states-religion. This figure includes Presbyterians from the Presbyterian Church (U.S.A.) as well as other Presbyterian denominations in the United States.

2. This statistic reflects survey respondents from all religious traditions, not just Presbyterians or Christians.

CHAPTER 25: YOU, ME, AND US

1. Names have been changed.

2. I use "mainline" here as "mainstream" is understood by Milton J. Coalter, John M. Mulder, and Louis B. Weeks in *Vital Signs: The Promise of Mainstream Protestantism* (Grand Rapids: Wm. B. Eerdmans Publishing Co., 1996; reprinted, Grand Haven, MI: FaithWalk Publishing, 2002). There, as here, it refers both to major American Protestant denominations such as American Baptist, Christian Church (Disciples of Christ), Episcopal Church (U.S.A.), Evangelical Lutheran Church in America, Presbyterian Church (U.S.A.), Reformed Church in America, United Church of Christ, United Methodist, as well as the discernable theological similarities among them (see xx–xxii). I use "evangelical" to describe students from generally nondenominational or independent churches, whose theology heavily emphasizes evangelism and personal salvation.

3. At other masses, I have participated more fully: reading prayers, offering blessings, and even preaching. But as a public face of Protestantism at the university, I choose not to receive the Eucharist at campus masses.

4. The study indicates that roughly 16 percent of Protestants have changed affiliation within Protestantism, and 51.3 percent of the adult population claim Protestantism overall, which is how I arrived at the one-in-three figure. For more information, see the Pew Forum on Religion and Public Life's *U.S. Religious Landscape Survey*, http://religions.pewforum.org/reports.

5. Though this "pure Christianity" stance is not a new phenomenon, it represents a frontier in ecumenism that will continue to be a challenge to future generations—and it is difficult to address through traditional conciliar and denominationally focused ecumenism.

6. John Macquarrie, *Christian Unity and Christian Diversity* (Philadelphia: Westminster Press, 1975), preface.

CHAPTER 26: WHENEVER YOU EAT THIS BREAD AND DRINK THIS CUP

1. The deacons of my congregation decided to send a chalice and paten to Sophia Presbyterian Church. That congregation now celebrates the Eucharist.

2. Hans Frei, "Response to 'Narrative Theology': An Evangelical Appraisal," *Trinity Journal* 8 (Spring 1987): 21–24.

3. Joseph Small speaks of six ecclesial implications when we realize our communion with the triune God, what he calls: "communion in faith, hope and love; communion in sacraments; communion in the truth of the gospel; communion in faithful living; communion in the reconciliation of differences; communion in patterns of mutual responsibility and accountability." "What Is Communion and When Is It Full?" *Reformed World* 56, no. 2 (June 2006): 165; originally published in *Ecclesiology* 2, no. 1 (2005).

4. Konrad Raiser, *Ecumenism in Transition: A Paradigm Shift in the Ecumenical Movement?* (Geneva: WCC Publications, 1991), 96.

5. Ibid., 97.

6. Ibid., 106.

7. Ibid., 107–8.

8. Ibid., 108.

9. Ibid., 109–11.

10. Ibid., 88.

11. Ibid., 114.

12. One of the most significant documents that tried to include all parts of Christianity was the monumental *Baptism, Eucharist, and Ministry*, Faith and Order Paper No. 111 (Geneva: World Council of Churches, 1982). The official responses of churches, including Reformed churches, to that document are Faith and Order Paper Nos. 129, 132, 135, 137, 143, 144. These correspond to vols. 1 through 6 of *Churches Respond to BEM: Official Responses to the "Baptism, Eucharist and Ministry,"* ed. Max Thurian (Geneva: WCC Publications, 1986–88). A number of Reformed churches, particularly in the global South, responded that while they appreciated a number of key steps toward theological convergence, they felt ignored by the process and product. In 2007, an Anglican theologian from Kenya, Prof. Jesse N. K. Mugambi, wrote an assessment at the 25th anniversary of the BEM document titled "Some Problems of Authority and Credibility in the Drafting and Reception Processes of the BEM Document," in *BEM at 25: Critical Insights into a Continuing Legacy*, ed. Thomas F. Best and Tamara Grdzelidze (Geneva: WCC Publications, 2007), 185–201. Mugambi amplifies the concerned responses of the Reformed churches and non-Reformed churches in the global South over what was seen as a disregard for the cultural and theological distinctive of particular contexts. The credible and relevant witness of the WCRC, like that of the BEM, will depend in large measure on the serious intentionality and creativity of the communion to connect the global-regional-local actors.

13. Though this has been asserted in works of liturgical theologians such as the late Roman Catholic scholar Aidan Kavanagh in *On Liturgical Theology* (New York: Pueblo Publishing Co., 1984) and the late Eastern Orthodox scholar Alexander Schmemann in *Introduction to Liturgical Theology* (Crestwood, NY: St. Vladimir's Seminary Press, 1966; 3rd ed., 1986), this notion of worship as the *esse* of the church's identity has been recently and most forcefully and lucidly discussed by Singaporean Pentecostal theologian Simon Chan in *Liturgical Theology: The Church as Worshiping Community* (Downers Grove, IL: InterVarsity Press, 2006). Chan states pointedly, "First, worship is what distinguishes the church as the church" (42).

14. In the context of Heb. 13:15–16, the term "sacrifice of praise" refers to the church's confession of Christ's lordship, as well as the acts of generosity and compassion offered to others.

15. These are three biblical metaphors that Chan highlights in discussing the church's "ontological relationship with the triune God"; *Liturgical Theology*, 24–40.

AFTERWORD: A NEW BOND IN A HIGHER CALLING

1. The full ecumenical affirmation is recorded in the *Minutes* of the 218th General Assembly, part 1, Presbyterian Church (U.S.A.) (Louisville, KY, 2008); also "The Ecumenical Stance of the Presbyterian Church (U.S.A.)," http://www.eif-pcusa.org/WhoWeAre/EIF-PCUSA VisionStatement.htm#policy.

2. WCC Executive Committee *Minutes*, February 18–20, 2003, WCC, Geneva, p. 30.

3. WCC Central Committee *Minutes*, February 15–22, 2005, WCC, Geneva, p. 126.

4. Sharon K. Youngs, "PC(USA) Urged to Keep Ecumenical Commitment," *Presbyterian News Service*, news release 07618, PC(USA), Louisville, KY, September 28, 2007; also at http://www.pcusa.org/pcnews/2007/07618.htm.

5. WCC Executive Committee *Minutes*, August 24–27, 2005, WCC, Geneva, p. 36.

6. Clifton Kirkpatrick and William H. Hopper Jr., *What Unites Presbyterians: Common Ground for Troubled Times* (Louisville, KY: Geneva Press, 1997), 161.